SPEAKING VOLUMES

A History of the
Cheltenham Festival
of Literature

NICOLA BENNETT

SUTTON PUBLISHING

First published in the United Kingdom in 1999 by
Sutton Publishing Limited · Phoenix Mill
Thrupp · Stroud · Gloucestershire · GL5 2BU

British Library Cataloguing in Publication Data

A catalogue record for this book is available from the British Library.

ISBN 0-7509-2249-4

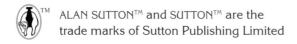

ALAN SUTTON™ and SUTTON™ are the
trade marks of Sutton Publishing Limited

Typeset in 10/15pt Korinna.
Typesetting and origination by
Sutton Publishing Limited.
Printed in Great Britain by
Redwood Books Ltd, Trowbridge, Wiltshire.

CONTENTS

Cheltenham Town Hall today, little changed since 1949. (Jon Gregson)

Imperial Square and the Queen's Hotel in the late 1940s. (Courtesy of Eric Franks A.R.P.S.)

1 THE FIRST IN BRITAIN

'I arrived in Cheltenham in 1949', said Joan Wilder, 'and I felt as if I'd come to the sticks. But that very week, there was a poster outside our little cottage: the Cheltenham Festival of Contemporary Literature. I went, and I have been to every festival since.' Every festival, that's fifty years, 395 days, 2,611 events and over 4,000 speakers. And words, too numerous to count.

In that time much has changed, but a lot has not. Almost every year the festival has taken place in Cheltenham Town Hall, an ornate Edwardian building in Imperial Square at the centre of what has always been the smart part of town. By 1949 an orchestra has been booked once more to play during the summer season. The chandeliers have been regilded and rehung, a new maple floor has been laid in the Main Hall, and plush tip-up chairs with ashtrays attached to alternate arms have been ordered for the auditorium. The organ has been cleaned and overhauled for the first time since 1938, and GEC have installed amplification apparatus complete with gramophone, turntable and wireless. Forty-five bicycle racks are now provided in the shrubbery between the Town Hall and the New Club, the gentlemen's club next door. Jitterbugging is officially banned, but takes place nevertheless. Most of the hotels have reopened after wartime requisitioning. Other icons of Cheltenham's past pleasures are being brought back to life: numbers are picking up at the Spa Baths, the Montpellier Rotunda, built as a spa, is to be opened to cater for the overspill of events from the Town Hall, and the graceful Pump Rooms in Pittville Park, used during the war for storage and quartering US troops, are being surveyed with a hopeful eye to their restoration as a cultural and social centre. After much municipal discussion it is decided that the Town Hall will provide refreshments – for large parties only, in order not to compete with local restaurants – and spa water will be served as ever from the ornate ceramic urns in the hall's 'Spa Well'.

It was in the Town Hall in 1945, only two or three weeks after the end of the war in Europe was celebrated – with open-air dancing, bands, a Punch and Judy show and donkey rides – that a most unusual phoenix rose from the ashes of the pre-war spa concert seasons: the first Cheltenham Music Festival. Thought up in 1944, it was G.A.M. Wilkinson, the Spa and Entertainments Manager, who convinced Cheltenham

Corporation that it would serve as an attraction to boost the fortunes of the town. The 'First Annual Festival' was planned to take place in July 1945 whether the war had finished or not, and with its emphasis on English music and new compositions it was a defiantly optimistic wave to the future. Benjamin Britten, William Walton and Arthur Bliss conducted a concert each with programmes that featured their own works, including the premières of two Britten pieces. The audience lapped it up belying anxieties that the programme might be too 'astringent' for popular taste. Arthur Bliss was delighted to see so many young people there and urged Cheltenham to 'Go all out on the festival idea'.

Those post-war years were famously culture hungry. By 1947 three successful music festivals had taken place. So far the Festival Committee had answered to the Town Improvement and Spa Committee of the Corporation, but it was becoming clear that this was not the most effective way of running an annual arts event. In addition the Arts Council of Great Britain, established in 1945 with one of its duties the subsidising of contemporary music, had given £100 to the festival in 1947 even though it was not allowed to give grants directly to local authorities. For future funding the festival needed to be separate. A proposal was drawn up for a non-profit-making limited liability company which would 'take over, carry on and develop the work of the Cheltenham Festival Committee'.

In the summer of 1948 Cheltenham Arts Festivals Ltd was formed for 'the promotion and encouragement of the Arts and in particular the Cheltenham Annual Festival and to organise, manage and conduct the Festival to include music, drama and such other forms of entertainment. . .'. Interestingly, the model implied by these words (which have since been changed) is that of one festival encompassing all the arts, echoing the Edinburgh Festival, which got going in 1947. In the setting up of Cheltenham Arts Festivals, the Corporation made sure it did not lose overall control. Its employees would be the administrators, and Borough Council members would make up the majority of its Board of Directors.

The first official mention of a sister festival dedicated to literature occurs in the minutes of the Town Improvement and Spa Committee for 13 April 1949. It is reported that speakers are to include Compton Mackenzie and C. Day Lewis, and the total cost is estimated at £300, which the Committee was assured would be 'recompensed by admission charges'. With financial liabilities set at nil, the report was approved.

Not mentioned by name is John Moore, the man who charmed and coerced his friends and club acquaintances into committing themselves to speak at the first-ever festival dedicated to the celebration of contemporary literature. In his introduction to the 1953 festival he was to describe the inception: 'More than five years ago George Wilkinson, the Spa Manager, asked for my advice about the planning and organisation of a Cheltenham Literary Festival in 1949. I was at first doubtful and indeed somewhat appalled. It had never occurred to me that a whole week of talks and similar solemnities would even half fill the big Town Hall. Moreover there had never been such a thing as a purely literary

The Municipal Offices and the Promenade, 1940s. (Courtesy of Eric Franks A.R.P.S.)

Latecomers hurrying past the New Club to the Town Hall . (Courtesy of Eric Franks A.R.P.S.)

festival in Britain before'. Lucile, John Moore's widow, still remembers the day when George Wilkinson, accompanied by Frank Littlewood, Cheltenham's Town Clerk, visited them at their house in Kemerton, a village on the flanks of Bredon Hill near Tewkesbury, to float the idea. Typically, John did not just offer advice, he committed himself. Lucile says 'I was upstairs in bed with flu. Had I been able to get up, I would have tried to dissuade him. John was *so* busy and he was quite incapable of saying no.'

Wilkinson and Littlewood had many good reasons for approaching John Moore. He was a well-known writer, riding high on the success of his recent book *Portrait of Elmbury*, a scarcely fictionalised account of Tewkesbury between the wars, and had just brought out two sequels to make it the Brensham Trilogy. He was local. He loved and understood the Gloucestershire countryside and the people who lived there. He was a generous spirited, convivial man, with a gift for talk – as happy at the bar of his local in Bredon as he was surrounded by the pick of raconteurs at the Savile, his London club. He was described by Peter Green, a fellow member, as ' among the best conversationalists I have ever known . . . and also a superb anecdotalist'. He knew masses of writers: C. Day Lewis, Stephen Spender, Eric Linklater, Nicholas Monsarrat, Ludovic Kennedy, T.H. White, Compton Mackenzie and C.S. Forester were all friends. Most directly relevant of all, John had hands-on experience of organising a festival. In the 1930s the vicar of Tewkesbury Abbey asked him to set about raising £25,000 to save the great bell tower, a task he achieved by putting on a summer season of mystery plays for several years.

His 1953 description of the genesis of a literary festival continues: 'In the usual English fashion we formed a committee. We sat late at our meetings and we talked hard; and generally a nucleus, if I may call it so, of the committee adjourned to a convenient pub after the meetings to continue the discussion there. Out of all this debate and criticism and fun (because there never was a less solemn committee) the pattern of a Literary Festival began to emerge. The pattern was roughly this: that we should begin with a serious address on some important and fairly general aspect of literature by someone of high repute: that thereafter we should allow our talks to range widely over the whole field covered by the written and spoken word – not concerning ourselves only with novels, poetry, biography and criticism, but also with drama, broadcasting, television, films and so on.'

Together, or so John – perhaps generously – would have us believe, they formulated the first programme: nine events spanning Monday 3 to Friday 7 October 1949. The eminent historian Arthur Bryant was to provide the first, meaty address in a talk examining 'The National Character'. Range would be supplied by the novelist and scriptwriter Nigel Balchin examining the relationship between film and the novel. Compton Mackenzie, sixty-six at the time and felicitously author of sixty-six published books, was to cover 'The Contemporary Novel', a contrast to the following day's talk by the youthful Emma Smith, who at twenty-five had won several awards for *Maiden's Trip*, her account of two years on working canal boats during the war. Ivor Brown, journalist and man of letters, educated at

John Moore.
(Courtesy of Lucile Bell)

Cheltenham College, was to deliver an address titled 'Words', C. Day Lewis had chosen a selection of contemporary verse to recite, and Peter Fleming, brother of Ian, would be speaking on 'Travel Writing'. The finale was 'Hurrah for Books!', devised and performed by Joyce Grenfell and Stephen Potter, well-known as a duo from their radio broadcasts. The whole thing was to be launched by Sir Ralph Richardson, a son of Cheltenham and the mayor's guest of honour at the inaugural lunch at the Queen's Hotel, just across Imperial Square from the Town Hall.

The *Gloucestershire Echo*, Cheltenham's local newspaper, devoted a full page to the festival. As well as publicising the programme, it took as its theme the pre-eminence of Cheltenham as home of the arts, particularly literature. 'There was a time, long ago, when all the leading novelists and poets could be met in its streets . . .'. Out of this fog of non-specific nostalgia emerge Jane Austen, Sir Walter Scott, Thackeray, Lord Byron and Alfred Tennyson. More recently, wrote the *Echo*, Cheltenham could claim John Masefield and James Elroy Flecker, son of the headmaster of Dean Close, one of the town's schools.

The paper scrupulously reviewed every event of the festival, starting with Ralph Richardson's opening: 'Describing himself as a jockey of literature – "the dramatist writes the plays and we try to make them run" – Sir Ralph toasted the prosperity of the Festival.' The occasion was for him a very happy return to his birthplace, he told the gathering,

Menu	*Toast List*
	"HIS MAJESTY THE KING"
Fillet of Sole Bonne Femme	Proposed by
	THE MAYOR OF CHELTENHAM
—	(Alderman P. T. Smith)
Roast Surrey Chicken	
Cauliflower Polonaise	Welcome to
Paysanne Potatoes	SIR RALPH RICHARDSON
	by
—	THE MAYOR OF CHELTENHAM
Peach Melba	Reply by
Petits Fours	SIR RALPH RICHARDSON
Coffee	MR. JOHN MOORE
	(Chairman of Literary Festival Committee)

Menu for the inaugural lunch at the Queen's Hotel, 1949.

adding: 'Whenever Cheltenham crops up in conversation I say with over-elaborate carelessness "As a matter of fact, I was born there" as if I owned the place.' Applause all round, welcome from the mayor, and a final word from John Moore, who recalled 'the time in the war when we both flew from the same air station'. What he did not mention was the background to Ralph's speech: 'If I do come to Cheltenham I shall be depending entirely on you to write a brilliant speech for me' was the reply sent in June to John's initial invitation.

There were problems. For Richardson to get to Cheltenham he needed petrol coupons: this entailed an application form so that the Town Clerk could apply to the Regional Petroleum Officer in Bristol. By September he was able to report: 'I have had a little present of petrol coupons and if there is anything over, I assure you I will share it with you behind the tent'. But there was still the speech. 'Everything is on the top line for this luncheon at Cheltenham on October 3rd except that I have not got a single line to say. You will send me something, won't you, and in good time'. It arrived, John was thanked most heartily, and the Literary Festival was off to a jolly start.

The next night the paper reported that Compton Mackenzie had received an ovation from a 'capacity' audience. The Main Hall holds about 1,000 people seated across the flat dance floor and above in the balconies. The stage is high so that people downstairs can see without raked seating and Compton Mackenzie stood alone at a lectern on the large stage, shared only with the best foliage and flowers Cheltenham Parks Department could offer. Mackenzie, whom Rosamund Lehmann said was the most brilliant speaker she had ever heard as well as a skilled mimic of the great men he had met in his time, beguiled Cheltenham completely.

Afterwards speaker, organisers and audience decamped to the Festival Club bar in the Pillar Room, one of the side rooms in the Town Hall.

G.A.M. Wilkinson.

The Main Hall today. The post-war colour scheme has gone, but otherwise much the same as the early days. (*Daily Telegraph*/Richard Watt)

Once installed Monty, as Mackenzie was called by friends, continued to regale his listeners, keeping them spellbound even though he had a habit of lapsing into silence at key moments in his anecdote to muse over his cigar or savour his drink. John Moore, his beautiful Australian wife Lucile and George Wilkinson, himself no slouch when it came to conversation, would have been circulating. Festival diehards unite in remembering the atmosphere at the Club (invented by the Music Festival in 1946) with enormous affection. Open to all, it encouraged audiences to mingle with performers for a couple of hours of egalitarian bonhomie, perhaps influenced by Savile Club principles – 'although all men may not yet be equal, all Savilians are equal'. Young women were warned to beware of hard-drinking poets, particularly Dylan Thomas, when he visited in 1950. They fell in love with his voice and humour, but the drink and his looks – a nightmare baby as one cruelly described him – kept them safely at a distance.

Emma Smith's talk entitled 'Why I Write' on the next evening has been remembered for fifty years as a high spot by one of the audience, who admired her down-to-earth articulacy and her pink cheeks and Dutch doll hairstyle. John Moore had written enthusiastically to Emma in 1948 after he read *Maiden's Trip*. In reply she told him his was her first fan letter. She agreed to his invitation to talk at the Festival 'with some considerable nervousness'. By the next letter, she is 'sick with terror' and on 8 August wrote 'I finished writing my Cheltenham talk today. The thought of delivering it fills me with the most acute alarm. I'm not at all sure that it isn't rubbish from one end to the other. I have no confidence in it. I feel on the brink of disgrace.'

In the event the talk seems to have been far from a disgrace. The newspaper report is full of appealing *aperçus* such as 'after spending the last two years of the war working on the canal, she found her mental energy and concentration being sapped by nostalgic recollections of that happy time. So she wrote a book about it – and thereby cast the clogging memories from her'. By 1953 Emma, who became a Cheltenham regular, could look back and write: 'I'm sure every year it gets better and better. But all the same, nothing could be nicer or more fun than that first time of all. O youth! O joy! O Cheltenham Literary Festival 1949!'

The first festival was hailed as a great success and according to the *Echo* 7,000 seats were filled. John Moore played down his own part and gave the credit to the audience (so good-humoured and appreciative), to George Wilkinson and staff, to the WVS who had supervised the publishers' book exhibition in the Drawing Room of the Town Hall, and to Mr Herdman, curator of Cheltenham Art Gallery and Museum, who had put on an exhibition of fine books of the previous century which included William Morris's Kelmscott *Chaucer*. All in all it was a fine beginning.

2 THE EARLY YEARS

Shortly before the second Festival of Contemporary Literature, John Moore received a letter inviting him to become an honorary vice-president of Cheltenham Arts Festivals, an honour the Board had created to recognise 'those who had contributed by their distinguished services to the undoubted success of the Festivals'. The letter pointed out that this invitation had been extended to one other only, namely Sir John Barbirolli, a similarly important figure for the Music Festival in the early years. John Moore, acting as chairman of the Literary Advisory Panel, was giving his services on a purely voluntary basis, and the Board wanted to do something to make it clear that they were properly grateful.

While Moore clearly enjoyed his baby, he probably had no intention or even idea at that time that he was destined to remain *in loco parentis* for the best part of the next thirteen years, in spite of what became increasingly serious efforts to unclasp its needy arms from his neck. Lucile says John always enjoyed the festival enormously, but laments that when one looked at the workload realistically it 'took three months out of his working year'. He was not a rich man and had to observe 'office hours' in order to make a living by writing articles, screenplays and short stories, and by becoming a regular broadcaster, as well as publishing a book almost every year. And yet for the next three years he programmed the festival largely single-handed.

If 7,000 seats were sold for the 1949 festival (and it seems a little unlikely), the figure was not matched by the subsequent three years. That first year the Main Hall was packed every evening. Emma Smith had the only small audience and, interestingly, it was not so much smaller than that for John Betjeman or Dylan Thomas the following year. But only the Brains Trust played to capacity in 1950, and the festival – probably to the organisers' horror – showed a loss. The Arts Council were approached to ask if they would consider offering a 'guarantee against loss' for the next one. As it turned out the 1951 box office takings were up again, perhaps influenced by 'big names' or perhaps by the razzmatazz of the Festival of Britain which swept both Cheltenham festivals under its wing. Although the festival did not need to draw on the promised grant in 1951, from now on it was to receive the interest and backing of the Arts Council until it was devolved to South West Arts in 1973.

Foyle's Literary Lunch – the celebrities in 1955: L.A.G. Strong, Christina Foyle, H.E. Bates, Lucile Moore and Compton Mackenzie. (Courtesy of the *Gloucestershire Echo*)

The formula had largely been set by the first year: eight or nine events at the Town Hall, scheduled for inside a week. During these years the National Book League took over responsibility for the publishers' book exhibition by arranging a display of 1,001 'Books of the Year' chosen from those published between the previous 1 June and 31 May. Penguin Books mounted a special display of their own. The opening lunch was not repeated, although in 1953 it was transmuted into a Foyle's Literary Lunch with a celebrity speaker, organised by the redoubtable Christina Foyle independently of the festival and to which performers – and even in later years directors – might or might not be invited.

The Festival Club was advertised as open 'for refreshments until 11 pm' (and in reality later, one suspects). Tickets for events were bookable and cost 3s 6d and 2s. The local secondary schools were much encouraged to send parties of students, and some teachers and heads were invited on to the Advisory Panel or to participate by chairing events and welcoming speakers.

One of the most stalwart supporters of both festivals from the beginning was Cyril Hollinshead, editor of the *Gloucestershire Echo*, who ensured that they were scrupulously covered by his reporters until he retired in the mid-1970s. One of them, novelist Barbara Hooper, remembers the early days well: 'Cheltenham in the early fifties was a fun place to live and work, and the fledgling Festival of Literature was a fun event. Festival groupies met almost every evening in the Festival Club. There the humblest *aficionado* could rub shoulders with distinguished authors, local worthies (and Cheltenham had aldermen in those days) as well as notables who came out of curiosity to see what it was all about. Members of Parliament seemed to be two a penny, and showbiz personalities added a touch of glamour in a largely pre-television era.'

Another highlight was the Brains Trust, which was introduced in 1950 and became the traditional conclusion to the festival for many years. Brains trusts were a popular phenomenon of the time – a panel of celebrities holding forth in response to questions submitted by the audience – to be found on the radio and in village halls up and down the country. Cheltenham's first was advertised as 'a new kind of literary brains-trust' and titled 'We Argue about Books', 'we' being Eric Linklater, the novelist E. Arnot Robertson and Emma Smith, kept in order by the BBC's Denis Morris. In the event Dylan Thomas joined them, and one suspects that another festival tradition in the making preceded their appearance: a very good dinner at a nearby hotel. One can see them on stage – man, woman, chairman, woman, man – lined up behind green baize, table microphones in front of them, ferocious spotlights showing up the massive dent on the front of Eric Linklater's bald head, acquired during the First World War, cigarette smoke wreathing the hall, each successive laugh raised more easily.

The *Echo* described it as a 'blithe finale . . . which produced delightful entertainment for a packed Town Hall audience. . . . The festive spirit was obviously present in the alert, versatile quartette . . . who provided conversation brimming with wit and humour. A striking divergence of approach and manner made the clash of personalities all the more animated.'

Arnot Robertson attributed the poor standard of contemporary criticism to a shortage of newsprint: 'Authors cannot live on their books since there is not enough paper, therefore they become book reviewers'. Dylan Thomas, 'when asked whether it was easier to understand a poet's face or his poetry, replied that he only looked at his face when he breathed on his mirror to see if he was dead.' Eric Linklater's response to 'Who do you think is the best of the three Powys brothers?' was (in sepuchral tones) 'If you can't hear me at the back it's because I have nothing to say'. And finally 'Answering a verbose, involved question on the duration of fame, Mr Thomas quipped characteristically: "The function of posterity is to look after itself."' (Who said it first? or was it he?) Facetiousness bordering on hilarity seeps between the lines of newsprint.

'Mr Thomas quipped characteristically'? How well did they know his quips? Quite well perhaps, because at 3 pm that day Dylan Thomas had given a 'rambling, wholly brilliant verbal firework display' on the subject of 'Light Verse' to a mixed audience of school children and adults. Prefacing his performance with the words 'I only read poems I like', Thomas invoked and declaimed poems by Hilaire Belloc, Robert Graves, W.H. Davies, Ezra Pound, W.H. Auden, Ogden Nash and John Betjeman in an 'effervescent flow of verse and comment, bubbling over with the spectacular talent of mimicry'. I have been

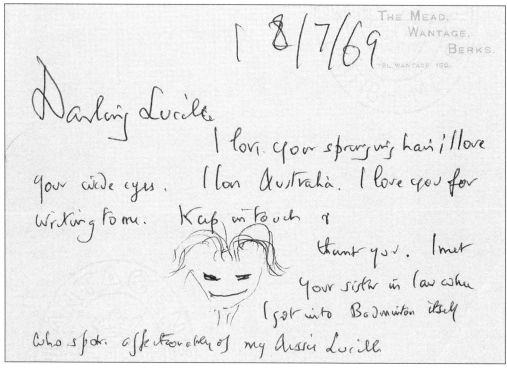

A characteristically ebullient note from John Betjeman addressed to Lucile Moore.

told of one schoolchild who never forgot that day and later became a poet. There would have been others converted to the cause, even if, as the *Echo* claimed, 'they had difficulty in distinguishing between verse-readings and extempore comment by the poet himself'.

As for Linklater's line, it must have got a big laugh because it is extremely unlikely that the sound was satisfactory. In that second year John Moore had felt it necessary to conclude his introduction to the publicity leaflet with the following words: ' The only thing which slightly marred our success last year was the faulty amplification, for which we sincerely apologise. The building is acoustically difficult, and although throughout the week we tried hard to improve upon our system of microphones and loud-speakers, we readily admit that we were never satisfied with the result. The trouble, however, has since been dealt with, and we are confident that you will now be able to hear clearly in all parts of the hall.' A 1949 letter from him refers to 'numberless complaints' received during the festival 'with regard to the amplifying equipment'. Unfortunately, this was *not* solved in 1950, but remained, particularly for panel events, a problem which continued to frustrate audiences and administration alike.

The next year, a microphone was introduced for the use of the Brains Trust audience when asking questions. John Moore's instructions were: 'if you put up your hand, a porter will bring you the travelling microphone and if it works, which is extremely unlikely, I shall be able to hear your question on the platform.' It didn't. Barbara Hooper remembers that the 1951 panel 'sparkled. . . . This in spite of the fact that the travelling mike, seen as a remarkable innovation, failed.' The panel this time consisted of Rose Macaulay, Georgie Henschel (daughter of the famous musician), Compton Mackenzie and John Betjeman.

John Betjeman had appeared the previous year to speak on Tennyson, having turned down an invitation to talk about light verse (presumably taken up by Dylan Thomas): 'Dear Moore', he wrote, 'I am not prepared to talk about light verse because I do not think my verse is so light as all that. . . . I can read my own verse or, alternatively, I can speak on Tennyson. I do not think there is anything else I can do.' Betjeman must have enjoyed Cheltenham as he returned, but even so he demurred, 'I don't much like the idea of Parlour Games, and would rather ask the audience questions instead.' In introducing him John Moore referred to his own description of himself as '"a miscellaneous writer"', and foremost among the miscellaneous matters on which he writes is of course architecture, in which his taste is individual and eccentric. He loves the nastiest railway stations, and during the war when so often I found myself stuck on the platform at Crewe or Stafford or Glasgow, I used to say to myself: "I wish John Betjeman were here instead of me".' John Betjeman became a good friend of the Moores, and his visits are well remembered by festival regulars. 'He opened our eyes to the Town Hall, which we hadn't really thought about before then', said one, and Lucile remembers him shocking the vicar of Tewkesbury Abbey with his enthusiasm over the Victorian rood screen.

Compton Mackenzie was 'back by popular demand'. Rose Macaulay, who had turned down an invitation to stay out at Kemerton because in Cheltenham 'I might get in a Brine Bath' (the only writer to mention such a thing – and was she joking in any case?), was reported to be in the process of writing a guidebook on ruins: 'the fact that she included the Cheltenham Festival in her itinerary is nothing to do with this.'

Sir Alfred Duff Cooper perhaps had an interest in common with Rose Macaulay for he arrived straight from a cure in Italy which forbade him spirits. Living in France, he was concerned about the price and quality of wine in England. Claret or champagne? Which was the safest choice? He gave the opening address on 'Literature and Politics'. A.P. Herbert gave an immensely popular talk on 'The British Laugh', Joyce Cary, author of *The Horse's Mouth*, talked about 'The Novel as a Picture of Society', and Val Gielgud, head of BBC Drama, first for radio and then for TV, suggested that the television play had the potential to be a new art form, distinct from either film or stage play.

The publicity leaflet is meticulous in giving titles, listing speakers' letters after their names, and in mentioning their war records, a reminder of how close it still was. The item for Thursday 4 October was billed 'Lt. Col. Robert Henriques MBE, on "Occupation – Writer"'. A description follows: 'Col. Henriques earns his living by his pen, though he was a professional soldier and is now a farmer as well as an author. During the war he served with the RA Commandos and in Combined Operations HQ, and was awarded the US Bronze and Silver Stars. Since then he has farmed at Bibury and consolidated his literary reputation with his long novel *Through the Valley*, which won the James Tait Black Memorial Prize this year.'

Not long after the 1951 Festival Robert Henriques received the following letter from John Moore:

I don't know whether you are back from France yet, but this is to ask you whether you would do me the great kindness of serving on my Cheltenham Festival Committee. It doesn't involve an awful lot of work – about seven or eight meetings a year, usually in the Town Hall, Cheltenham at 5 o'clock on days which we fix as far as possible to suit everybody. As a matter of fact, we get quite a lot of fun out of it. So do say yes if you feel you can spare the time. You will get an official letter from the Cheltenham Corporation.

A note is inscribed at the top, 'Ans. Yes, provisionally'.

Like John Moore, Henriques was a writer, a regular broadcaster and reviewer, a member of the Savile and a true countryman. They may have first met in the war, certainly they were both involved in the plans for the top secret 'Mulberry Harbour' operation. It is clear that John Moore was keen to get a like mind with contacts on to the Advisory Panel. The minutes of the first meeting Henriques attended, held in January 1952, allow us to see what ideas were in the air for the next festival: T.S. Eliot and Augustus John are to be approached as opening speakers; for a talk on film illustrated by excerpts they will try for Carol Reed or failing him Roy Boulting; other speakers hoped for include Graham Greene, Dorothy L. Sayers, H.E. Bates and Peter Ustinov; and among those recommended for the Brains Trust are Dilys Powell, Ralph Richardson, Dr J. Bronowski, Gilbert Harding, Freddy Grisewood and Ralph Wightman, the last three Savile Club cronies.

Robert Henriques in the farmyard at Bibury. (W.R. Bawden)

The next letter from John makes it clear that he and Henriques are to share negotiations with potential speakers. Henriques is to approach the film-makers, they are both to work on the Brains Trust team ('Do you know Marghanita Laski, who is so often on TV she might perhaps be a draw? We want one or two more girls anyhow, preferably decorative ones'). The 'nos' come in: Eliot, Greene (out of the country), Sayers, Carol Reed will be filming in California, Roy Boulting will think about it, H.E. Bates is booked to see friends in Switzerland. On to new ideas. The letters go back and forth. Moore to Henriques: 'Daphne du Maurier apparently makes it a

LITERARY FESTIVAL PERSONALITIES.—Mr. Charles Morgan (centre), the speaker at the opening night of the fourth Cheltenham Festival of Contemporary Literature at the Town Hall, Cheltenham, last night. On left is Col. Robert Henriques, who presided, and on right Mr. John Moore (chairman of the Festival).

Cutting from the *Cheltenham Chronicle and Gloucestershire Graphic*, 7 October 1952.

rule never to speak at any meetings – I suppose she can well afford to'. 'Sad to say I heard from Augustus John today and he will not come. Will you now please try Charles Morgan for us? Better mention that fee of £25 is in no way related to speaker's name or reputation.' Charles Morgan says yes. Marghanita Laski too. Ralph Richardson will come if his stage engagements permit. Lord David Cecil will talk about Shakespeare's comedies. Dilys Powell wants to give a lecture on 'The Critic at the Cinema' rather than appear on the Brains Trust panel. Nevill Coghill, who produced three of the Tewkesbury Abbey plays for John Moore in 1935, has agreed to speak on 'Chaucer's View of Women'. Charles Morgan wants to give a lecture called 'Liberties of the Mind'. Will this title be offputting for the Cheltenham audience? The Brains Trust is fixed: Gilbert Harding will chair, Rex Warner and Ralph Wightman will be balanced by decorative women Frances Day and Marghanita Laski. And C. Day Lewis has stepped in give a poetry reading with his new wife Jill Balcon. There are fears that the last may be a bit highbrow, but the festival has been offered £250 by the Arts Council to promote poetry, so the event cannot make a loss. There: the publicity can go out. George Wilkinson at the Town Hall, still in the aftermath of the Music Festival, which takes place in July, needs to rush it all to the printer.

September, and Robert Henriques is offering many of the line-up accommodation at his Cotswold farmhouse. He can promise his guests a good day's shooting, as well as an excellent cook and a passable cellar. Several of the speakers write to ask if they should wear evening dress for their appearances.

The resulting festival was hailed as the most successful ever. John Moore wrote proudly to Robert Henriques 'Our profit was £51'. The poetry evening turned out to be packed.

Gilbert Harding excelled as chair of the Brains Trust, because of or despite his declaration, 'I don't intend at all just to sit here and put questions. I may say I have always avoided the two main vices – moderation and tolerance.'

This was corroborated by a little local furore. Harding wrote an article for the *People* which mocked the Ellenborough Hotel – hosts of the now traditional pre-event dinner for the Brains Trust – for the quality of its oxtail soup and for having the pretension to call it 'Potage de queue de boeuf'. The hotel's proprietor Margaret Davies sent an indignant letter of response:

> Oxtails are difficult for even hoteliers to obtain but our butcher does occasionally let us have two which will serve about twelve people when braised. On October 10th we were able to buy one oxtail and used it to make soup for sixty people.
>
> The soup was made 'with loving care' and chef and I hoped that, as we were serving Gilbert Harding, it would be particularly good. We were both very sorry that it was merely food for adverse criticism.

Robert Henriques apologised fulsomely: 'I am most sorry that he should have behaved in such an offensive and ridiculous manner. . . . My wife and I are enthusiastic connoisseurs of food and wine ourselves . . . and she and I agreed that we could not have got a better meal anywhere in England.' Margaret Davies must have been appeased for she remained one of the festival's staunchest supporters, providing meals and accommodation at special rates. Festival performers remember Ellenborough dinners to this day: the good talk that sped them from the soup through late arrivals to the scraping back of chairs and the lighting of cigarettes. Eventually coffee cups, glasses and lipstick-stained napkins were abandoned and the sound of voices would recede down the street to the Town Hall and the expectant crowd that awaited them.

3 A CONTEMPORARY FESTIVAL?

At George Wilkinson's suggestion Robert Henriques' name was put on the festival's letterhead as Deputy Chairman of the Advisory Panel to John Moore's Chairman. The quantity of letters that were written in 1953 are testimony to a new burst of energy for the festival. It was a difficult year for John: he had a novel to finish in August and the Moores were trying to sell their house in Kemerton and planning to go abroad. He was clearly grateful to Robert for taking on some of the burden at a busy time, and from their letters they both patently enjoy the fun of being 'conspirators in arms'.

Both men are talked of with affection by 1950s festival-goers, who remember them as excellent hosts on stage and off. If John was the one everyone loved – approachable and ready to help – Robert's rather county manner combined with his Hispano-Jewish good looks gave him the edge on glamour. The fragments of autobiography which his daughter Veronica Gosling published after his death reveal him as possessed of a laceratingly self-critical inner voice, perhaps the scars of schoolboy misery and humiliation at Rugby. But, as one of his friends protested to Veronica, 'this is not Robert as he was', and to the outside world he appeared an immensely talented, fun, fiery man who enjoyed life in all its intensities. Like Gilbert Harding (who became, partly due to the festival, a family friend), Robert would not have claimed to be a tolerant person. His hackles rose particularly at any kind of official ineptitude. Privileged by background and upbringing, he was yet an instinctive champion of the weak and the under-appreciated.

Ideas for the 1953 festival flowed freely. Suggestions for the opening speaker seem to have been even more ambitious than usual: Evelyn Waugh, Winston Churchill, Somerset Maugham and E.M. Forster were on the initial list. This may partly have been because Robert had suggested inviting a French author, which was taken in some quarters of the Panel as a direct insult to the quality of the homegrown product. More moderate voices expressed concern that unless this was a French writer with excellent English he might not be audible.

As it turned out the festival was opened by St John Ervine, seventy-year-old Ulsterman, playwright and critic. Early on Moore updated Henriques: 'All my lines of approach to Winston suggest he will not come. . . . Likewise Maugham. I shall not, however, approach

Snapshot from Veronica Gosling's album showing John Moore, her mother Vivien, a friend Ninette Montague and St John Ervine at the Henriques' during the 1953 festival.

Forster until after the next meeting. . . . I would rather you tried, with even the remotest chance of success, Evelyn Waugh. Will you please, therefore, do this before you go? You will probably get a frightful raspberry, as I did two years ago.' The response was: 'Evelyn Waugh: He is at present abroad and I think it would be fatal to shoot a letter into the pile that will be awaiting his return. Easily the best chance of success is to ask him personally in a mellow mood. We usually dine together once or twice a year . . . and I will take occasion to do so . . . I really believe this is the best bet, even though the odds are still sternly against us.' As indeed it turned out.

St John Ervine was described vividly by John Moore in a letter to the editor of *Promenade*, a local weekly arts sheet started that year: '[He] is one of the most combative persons that I have ever met. He is lame from his first war wound and walks with a stick. When he is arguing his hair seems to stand up like a cock's comb and I always feel he will use the stick to reinforce his argument. He was one of Shaw's best friends – and greatest admirers which is odd because their views about almost everything must have been so very different.'

Another event that needed some sorting out was the debate between C.P. Snow and his wife, the novelist Pamela Hansford Johnson. Moore to Henriques: 'I enclose a copy of his [Snow's] letter from which you will see that he doesn't want to call it a debate because he and his wife most miraculously agree about everything – a state which I had not previously known to exist this side of heaven. What on earth shall we call it?' In the end they stuck to their guns and called it 'An Argument', discarding 'Is there a New Movement in Literature?' which Snow had suggested.

Hopes of luring Edith Sitwell to appear were dashed by a letter headed Sunset Tower, Hollywood: 'I am here doing what they call the "treatment" of a film, and my director tells me I shall probably have to return here about the dialogue.' Hollywood and Edith Sitwell; one can imagine those distinctive English vowels cutting through the sunlight on a Californian hillside: 'We are having a heat wave here – 80° in the shade, and an outbreak of rabies. I think the afflicted dogs must have been bitten by the gossip columnists, whose conduct is unbelievable. Yours sincerely, Edith Sitwell.'

For the Brains Trust, John Moore secured his old friend Ludovic Kennedy and his wife, the dancer Moira Shearer, to appear with Jennie Lee and others. Earlier in the week Stephen Spender, 'mild, equivocal and erudite', as *Promenade* chose to describe him, spoke on D.H. Lawrence, and attempted the tricky task of explaining his mystical beliefs. Ironically, the event that attracted the smallest audience was probably the one that the programmers would have expected to have most popular appeal: a panel discussion on *The Archers.* A surreal note creeps in here: the author of *Mrs Dale's Diary,* another long-running radio soap, by chance contacted the festival because she wanted Mrs Dale's fictional son-in-law, a publisher by trade, to visit it that year. On receiving the programme, she wrote to John Moore: 'We were entertained to find that our rivals "The Archers" were figuring in it, I hope Mrs Dale's son-in-law will not make a scene.'

In 1953 Cheltenham held a poetry competition for the first time. This was later reincarnated in more than one guise – the Guinness Poetry Competition, the *Telegraph Magazine* Poetry Competition, the *TLS* Poetry Competition. At that time there seems to have been a desire to make the festival more local, which resulted in the competition being open only to Gloucestershire poets or to writers of poems about Gloucestershire. This was in the face of disapproval from the Arts Council, whose money was going into the festival on the basis of its being a national event.

All competitors were to submit their poems under a pseudonym and Richard Church, poet, ex-civil servant and at the time director of the English Festival of Spoken Poetry (described more informally by John Moore as 'a verray parfait gentil poet except when he is playing against me at snooker when the savager side of his nature comes out'), would act as judge.

Interestingly Richard Church awarded both first prizes – 'sonnet' and 'any other poem' – to the same person, a young woman from Nailsworth who chose not to reveal her real identity, but was also the author of a recently published novel that Robert Henriques had admired. Henriques, fascinated by the coincidence, took up her cause by recommending her book to several of his contacts in the literary world.

The other poet to receive their encouragement was Sidney E. Knight, who comes off the page of his letters as a character quite colourful enough for the Brensham Trilogy. Now living in South Africa, he sent in a long poem called 'Gloucestershire Exile' which brought the house down. It was later performed on the BBC Home Service and published by the festival, all through the offices of the chairmen, both of whom conducted lengthy correspondences with the exile.

Peggy Ashcroft and John Laurie were persuaded to perform the competition-winning poems sandwiched between better-known poems about Gloucestershire under the title 'A Recital of Gloucestershire Poetry'. The programme as printed in the illustrated handbook, another first for the festival of that year, is not accurate. A letter from Peggy Ashcroft firmly outlines the ten alterations she proposes to make to the selection, John Laurie had as many, and Richard Church decided he'd like to read some of the competition sonnets himself. With but a moan or two off-stage (after all, he had said they could change poems they did not like), John Moore assembled a revised list.

Particular efforts were made to involve schools that year. An idea had been floated by Robert Henriques of 'student members' attending informal discussions sessions, but the panel dismissed it on practical grounds. There remained a determination to consult the schools – Pate's Grammar School for Girls, Cheltenham Grammar School, The Ladies' College, Dean Close and Cheltenham College among them – about the speakers they would like to hear. The festival even thought about inviting Enid Blyton as a draw for the under-fourteens. A couple of years later Elizabeth Browning, the wife of a Cheltenham College master, partly realised Henriques' idea by giving informal lunch parties for twelve pupils from the schools to meet the writers.

The chairman's introduction to the 1953 handbook explained how the festival started. The deputy chairman's contribution looked to the future rather than the past: 'We have the same problem as the publisher. We know we can make a little money on a best-selling

Gloucestershire Poetry event 1953: John Laurie, Peggy Ashcroft and Richard Church about to go on stage. (Courtesy of the *Gloucestershire Echo*)

writer who can fill the Town Hall any day with people anxious to hear him. How are we to tempt those same people . . . to buy seats to listen to somebody whose writings, in our opinion, make him worthy of our platform but whose name is scarcely known to the public?' The answer he offers is that 'We must be closely in league with the audiences. . . . Mutually we must make the festival imprint a guarantee of distinction, so that anyone who buys a seat . . . can know for sure that it will be worth the money.

'Our Festival aim – which we cannot hope to secure immediately – must be an interchange of views between platform and audience, writer and reader, critic and publisher and librarian and bookseller and buyer of books. This would make a real festival of contemporary literature.'

He feels that one way of bringing promising writers to public attention is through competitions: 'Next year I think we should start a prize for the best "first novel" to be published in the previous twelve months.'

Indeed, plans were under way as soon as the 1953 festival had been formally put to bed. In November the Advisory Panel met for this purpose and later celebrated with a dinner at the Ellenborough. The day before John Moore, keen that it be a good evening and concerned that some of his members might find the cost a bit steep, wrote to his deputy chairman: 'I wonder whether you would mind going halves with me in the drinks before Dinner? . . . We can call it the Chairmen's Privilege.' His letter the next day started: 'I thought it was a very good evening last night. I had a hangover this morning.'

This didn't prevent him from getting down to business: 'I have . . . written to Emma Smith about the Novel Competition and I should be grateful if you would write to David Cecil and Charles Snow.' John, Robert, Emma Smith and C.P. Snow were to be the judges with Lord David Cecil their chairman. The conditions of the competition were drawn up: 'First Prize £50 (with two Commendations of £5 each) for a first novel of high literary merit published between October 1st 1953 and September 30th 1954, to be submitted by the publisher in proof or print by June 1st.'

Reports and letters started to come in. The chairmen battled with the logistics of exchanging books and opinions. In May Moore wrote to Henriques: 'You had better keep these copies of Emma's comments which although I don't agree with all of them strike me as extremely acute and percipient. You will adore her.' As the months went by it became apparent that the front runners were *Under the Net* by Iris Murdoch, *Hackenfeller's Ape* by Brigid Brophy and *Lucky Jim* by Kingsley Amis.

On these books the judges were fairly unanimous, but each harboured a less popular favourite. Emma's was *The Violins of Saint-Jacques* by Patrick Leigh Fermor, 'a period piece set in 1902 in the French island of Saint-Jacques in the Antilles', as John described it. C.P. Snow remained loyal to a book he had liked from the beginning: *The Goodly Seed* by John Wyllie, a documentary-style account of survival in a Japanese prisoner of war camp. Henriques was attracted to an unsettling book called *Brotherly Love* by Gabriel

Fielding, a prison doctor who wrote under a pseudonym. And a book that arrived late from Faber and was sent to Charles Snow for initial assessment received no more than a line: 'Rejected out of hand.' It was *Lord of the Flies* by William Golding.

To David Cecil, who had read all the books his judges felt worthy of the trouble, fell the task of extracting a final judgement. It was agreed that the panel would dine in his rooms at New College, Oxford, at the end of July. But the day before: 'I am afraid that it is quite impossible for me to get to Oxford on Thursday night. I am so sorry', wrote Charles Snow. He put his views on paper for them: 'My own choice is first prize: *The Goodly Seed*. Commendations: *Lucky Jim, Hackenfeller's Ape*. . . . If the four of you are agreed on a choice entirely different from mine, write to me and I will acquiesce if I can bend my conscience as far as it will go. If I can't acquiesce, then I can silently disappear from the committee. It is very difficult to make this kind of choice; I would have thought the main consideration was to avoid choosing a book which none of us much likes but which no one actively dislikes.'

After the Oxford evening, it fell to John Moore to write with characteristic tact and tell the absentee what happened. They had quickly agreed that the choice for first prize lay

The First Novel Competition 1953/4: judges Emma Smith and David Cecil with prizewinners Iris Murdoch and Brigid Brophy. (Courtesy of the *Gloucestershire Echo*)

between *The Goodly Seed, Hackenfeller's Ape, Lucky Jim, Under the Net* and *The Violins of Saint-Jacques. Lucky Jim* was dropped because after initial enthusiasm they felt the more lasting impression was 'a curiously chilly one'. Without its advocate present *The Goodly Seed* went, because – and here they bore in mind Snow's caveat – 'none of us would have been really *enthusiastic* about it'. *The Violins of Saint-Jacques* had the support of Emma, Robert and David Cecil, but it was thought that 'you would not be able to accept this and I should have had difficulty in doing so'. Moore went on:

> We were left with *Under the Net* and *Hackenfeller's Ape.* There was great support for the former. I was felt that of the two it was the perhaps the richer book. The characters had a more independent existence, the writing perhaps had more guts and vitality. Against this *Hackenfeller* was perhaps more a true work of the imagination, a more perfect though possibly a slighter thing. It was such a near shave between these two books that we decided to give an additional second prize of £20. By the narrowest of margins we chose *Hackenfeller* first and *Under the Net* second and David Cecil said he would be happier if the two books were placed in this order.
>
> We decided also to give an additional commendation so the prize list reads (1) *Hackenfeller's Ape*, (2) *Under the Net*; Commendations: *Lucky Jim, The Goodly Seed, The Violins of St Jacques.*

Charles Snow's conscience did not bend. He quietly (and amicably, John Moore made sure of that) dipped out of the team and the Judges' Report in the 1954 handbook makes no mention of his name.

One wonders how much the awards meant to the recipients, who as it turned out were good friends. Iris Murdoch wrote hastily when she got back from a summer in Italy. No letter survives from Brigid Brophy; only from her father, the novelist John Brophy, and mother, who were keen to attend. A member of the audience told me: 'they were real bluestockings. I remember Iris Murdoch's fair hair cut short in a fringe. She wore a bright yellow satin blouse and a black skirt. I was quite in awe of such amazing girls. Lord David Cecil was a wonderful chairman, very enthusiastic. I can see him now, bouncing up and down in his chair. ' Presumably Kingsley Amis and confrères got their £5s in the post.

4 THE DIE IS CAST

The coup of the 1954 festival was the appearance of André Maurois, whom Robert Henriques approached when he visited Paris as one of six English writers invited to a 'Kermesse aux Etoiles', part of a year of celebrations dedicated to the *Entente Cordiale*. There were still doubts – would a French writer attract an audience? audibility, and so on. John Moore thought there were only two French writers who would fill or half-fill the Town Hall: 'André Maurois who I imagine is very old and François Mauriac who cannot be very young. Sartre might have got a moderate audience largely out of curiosity three or four years ago but I rather feel his fame is on the decline. So there we are: Maurois or Mauriac.'

Maurois was an anglophile who had served in both wars as a liaison contact with the British army, which may have predisposed him towards Col. Henriques. He was an excellent choice for Cheltenham: his English was perfect, Harold Nicolson had called him 'the leading biographer of our age', he had written almost as many books about English writers – Shelley, Byron, Disraeli – as he had about his own countrymen – Voltaire, Proust, Georges Sand, Victor Hugo. His letters are charming, to the point and utterly lacking in self-importance. He was to come over with his wife Simone (née de Caillavet and the model for Proust's Mlle de Saint-Loup), Robert would meet them at the airport, they would stay with the Henriques, they would see *Romeo and Juliet* at Stratford together as the guests of Anthony Quayle, and . . . he was at the festival's disposal, but as they were old would like to have the mornings to rest.

Most of his opening address 'The Philosophy of Reading' was printed in the following year's handbook. He began 'Books are better and wiser than their authors. . . . Even the most brilliant talker cannot be, on the spur of the moment, as brilliant as he is in meditation.' For after all 'the spoken word is soon forgotten. . . . A great book, or work of art, are the only friends we can come back to, day after day, to ask them their secret.'

The year 1954 was one of more than the usual number of changes at the last minute. The historical novelist Margaret Irwin had been billed to speak on 'History as Fiction' on 5 October. She had been so keen on the programme that she had booked her sister and herself into a hotel to stay the whole five days, but her next letter, dated 4 October, was written from hospital, where she was seriously ill. The festival must have had some prior

André Maurois charms admirers in the Festival Club, 1954. (Courtesy of the *Gloucestershire Echo*)

warning because A.L. Rowse is advertised in her slot. However, he seems not to have thought highly of historical fiction which he referred to as 'a hybrid for art' and firmly titled his own talk 'History as Literature'.

Eric Linklater, who had been rounded up for all sorts of events – a debate, a talk for schools – was the other casualty. He was an old friend of John's, whom the Moores often visited at his home in Nigg. His letters were always highly colourful, and he was known to terrify strangers on trains and novice members of the Savile Club by the fierceness of his gaze. His initial response to John's idea of a schools' talk was quick:

This is an outrageous idea!

I account you a friend, and now you propose to throw me to a savage battalion of teen-agers to be howled at, pelted, jeered at – heaven knows what. Who do you think I am? Sinatra? However, I have not yet tried the power of my glittering eye on such an audience, and a new experience has always attracted me . . .

But it never happened for, according to the paper which praised his substitute Marghanita Laski, he was ill. Perhaps the prospect overwhelmed him after all.

Another reluctant speaker was Christopher Fry, whom John had been trying to persuade to Cheltenham for several years. As it turned out he gave a superb lecture titled 'Why Verse', so good that extracts were printed in the 1955 handbook. And the Brains Trust was as popular as ever, with a team of 'radio and literary personalities' including Malcolm Muggeridge. Despite cancellations the festival was again hailed as 'the most successful ever'.

The Brains Trust team in 1954: Robert Henriques, Marghanita Laski, Malcolm Muggeridge, A.G. Street, Lady Isobel Barnett and John Moore. (Courtesy of the *Gloucestershire Echo*)

The letters between Moore and Henriques show they had become real friends: they are funny, teasing, supportive, rude about each other and others, efficient and sympathetic. As usual they were under some pressure: both were writing novels and Robert had recently taken on the neighbouring 1,000-acre farm. By September he was desperately working to rescue the harvest from disaster, and there was tension brewing at Cheltenham Arts Festivals.

The festival was now one of the Arts Council's regular clients, annually awarded a grant offered in the form of a guarantee against loss. Nevertheless it took pride in the fact that so far the money had not been needed. Cyril Wood, Regional Director and official representative on the Board and the Literary Advisory Panel, Eric W. White, Assistant Secretary-General, and Joseph Compton, Chairman of the Poetry Panel, were all on friendly and supportive terms with the festival. That year, because they were keen to help build its profile in the media, the Arts Council allowed them to hold their first-ever London press party at their offices in St James's Square.

Handsome invitations in grey and maroon to match the style of the festival handbook were sent out. Willy-nilly Henriques and Moore found themselves bogged down in the details of catering and guest lists. The Town Hall caterers were reluctant to provide canapés, staff or glasses. A letter from John, handwritten in the absence of his secretary Diana, is an indication of their predicament (or John's, anyway): 'I am miserable about Diana. I can't find anything. The telephone keeps going, and I am trying to write my novel. Why do we do this festival? George Wilkinson tells me "the Mayor is against it". The Council made every difficulty about supplying staff for our London party so . . . we are borrowing four pretty waitresses from Diana's mother's café. Lucile is doing all the eats. The Town Hall after much hesitation has reluctantly agreed to supply the glasses.' He adds gallantly, 'But all these troubles are very trivial compared with your harvest.'

Robert's publisher David Farrer of Secker and Warburg congratulated them afterwards: 'What a grand and enjoyable party that was the other evening! . . . I do seriously think you and John Moore have done and are doing a most valuable job in organising the Cheltenham Festival. It goes from strength to strength and really helps to vitalize the publishing and book trades.'

Immediately after this festival Joseph Compton wrote to Moore:

I came away from Cheltenham more deeply impressed than ever by what you and Robert Henriques are doing. . . . You have created something of real importance and I know that the Arts Council support me wholeheartedly in my view of the value and possibilities of your Festival.

I had a short talk with Robert about the difficulties and distresses you were experiencing in your dealings with the Corporation. I suggested to him that the time had come when a Festival Trust should be formed which would give stability and ensure continuity.

On his return to London, he continued, he had had a word with W.E. Williams, the Secretary-General, and reported that he too was strongly in favour of a Trust. 'I am certain that in planning for the future of the Festival you can rely on the support of the Council in every way they can give it.'

A hiccough in the arrangements had unfortunately prevented the mayor from speaking at the festival. Despite George Wilkinson's comments, he said in a letter that he had wanted to thank them publicly on behalf of the Borough.

There they had it – a locally and nationally recognised institution with a future, respected by public, publishers, authors and arts establishment alike.

The laurels had scarcely had time to wither on their brows before another letter arrived, this time from Frank Littlewood, the Town Clerk and Secretary of Cheltenham Arts Festivals. It was such a masterful piece of circumlocution that it had John Moore baffled, 'but I think the gist of it is that we take too much upon ourselves in making decisions on our own and carrying them out personally instead of through the correct bureaucratic channels', he wrote to Robert. He was right. The Board felt themselves financially responsible for a festival over which in practice they felt they had no control. 'One of the things you will no doubt be thinking over is whether the Festival would not do better with a separate organisation.' Frank Littlewood must have got wind of the talks with the Arts Council. 'I feel perfectly sure that there are ways and means of relieving you of much of the detail you have so courteously and generously undertaken in the past.' And heard of their complaints about having to do so much of the work.

John replied to the effect that their autonomy was by no means complete. Their meetings were minuted, estimates and accounts were submitted to the Arts Council via the Board. They had to get approval for unusual expenditure, for example the press conference. Where they did act independently was in planning the programme, deciding on fees for the speakers and on all matters concerning publicity. The Panel met to consider such matters, but between times it had to be a matter of individual discretion. 'The point is that these things have to be done on a personal basis. It is very often a matter of seeing a particular writer in my club and seizing the opportunity of saying "Look here old boy, will you come down to Cheltenham?"'

Four days later Henriques and Moore met White and Compton in London and discussed further the idea of a trust which would organise the festival as a national event taking place, if the Corporation backed it, in Cheltenham.

The chairmen's ideas were presented to the Advisory Panel. The festival would be called the 'English Literary Festival' and twelve trustees would include representatives from all the literary institutions and from educational bodies. Their ideas were met with tentative approval. On behalf of the Borough Council Frank Littlewood raised no objections, although he thought it might take a long time to set up a trust. Later the Panel endorsed their proposals in a written response to the Town Clerk's memorandum.

Meantime it was clear that Robert and John were not entirely in accord. Robert, the idealist and planner, was all for wiping the slate clean. John was more pragmatic. He was unwilling to go so far as to dispense with the panel and radically change the way the festival was administered. Robert dreamt of a secretariat of their own and independence from the Town Hall and the Corporation – a shedding of all forms of that irksome bureaucracy that went against his grain. But they left it that John would speak for them both at the next panel meeting as Robert was going away. It would not be a problem as things seemed to be going their way.

On the evening John sensed that something was up. The Panel had turned out in unusual force. Littlewood, always an ebulliently good-humoured man, seemed even better pleased than usual, and he had brought his assistant with him. John opened the meeting and had hardly announced the second item, 'The Reconstitution of Cheltenham Arts Festival Ltd', when the Town Clerk interrupted him to say that he and his assistant happened to have spoken to W.E. Williams, Secretary-General of the Arts Council. He reported with evident pleasure that it was Williams' opinion that there there was no need to change the name of the festival, and that in view of the Borough's fine record as a supporter of the arts, really no need at all for the formation of a trust. John avoided putting the ensuing discussion to the vote. He knew that it would result in 9 votes against the trust and 1 for – his own. The Town Clerk had succeeded in completely wrong-footing him.

The next day John received a letter from a member of the Panel. 'I think the root of this is that the Board of Directors has . . . never yet noted the difference between us and the Music Festival. I thought it significant that several times, at our meeting the other night, the phrase was used that they pay the piper and may therefore call the tune. That, of course, is (literally) what they do for the Music Festival, which is necessarily a professional affair. . . . The Literary Festival is essentially an amateur affair. . . . Nobody with a grain of sense would suppose that our best speakers appear for the trifling sums we are able to pay them. Persuading those men and women to appear is an enterprise vastly different from the engaging of professional musicians for the Music Festival; and the ability to do so does not lie in the Board of Directors.'

The Board did not agree to the Literary Festival moving outside the control of the Company and the Council. Moore and Henriques were for the Trust. They resigned, but Moore agreed to go to a meeting at the Arts Council in his private capacity only. He wrote to Robert, 'in the end I got the following offer out of them which seems to fulfil most, though not all, of the conditions we made': in short the company would be somewhat reconstituted so that more members of the Board could be elected from outside the Borough Council, the Literature Festival would be allowed to act autonomously apart from a yearly submission of budgets and accounts, a society would be formed for festival supporters, and a council formed of representatives from national literary and educational bodies. The Advisory Panel would become a management committee which would work with the festival director (or directors).

With much behind-the-scenes negotiation, John Moore persuaded Robert Henriques to accept this formula, and they agreed to become co-directors of the 1955 Cheltenham Festival of Contemporary Literature.

Cyril Wood, perhaps making amends, busied himself with setting up the Festival Society which was launched on 13 April by J.B. Priestley, who had forgotten or revised his opinion of five years before: 'I doubt if a literary festival is really possible. Literature is from a writer to a reader and has nothing public about it. Unlike music and drama, which are communal arts.' Wood prevailed upon an old friend of his, Noel Newman, a local businessman, to become chairman and George Dowty, head of one of Cheltenham's biggest industries, was approached for president.

Dowty put up the money for a travelling scholarship for a young writer to go to Canada, and he was keen to put his considerable energies at the disposal of the festival. With his encouragement a public relations officer was employed (not very successfully – the

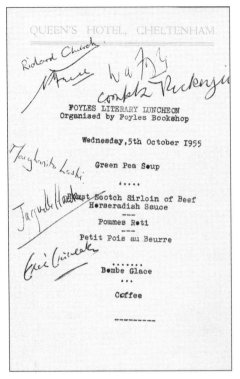

QUEEN'S HOTEL, CHELTENHAM

Richard Church

FOYLES LITERARY LUNCHEON
Organised by Foyles Bookshop

Wednesday, 5th October 1955

Green Pea Soup

· · · · ·

Roast Scotch Sirloin of Beef
Horseradish Sauce

———

Pommes Roti

———

Petit Pois au Beurre

· · · · · ·

Bombe Glace

· · ·

Coffee

—————————

Foyle's Literary Luncheon, 1955: menu signed by speakers J.B. Priestley and Jacquetta Hawkes and guests of honour Marghanita Laski, Eric Linklater, Compton Mackenzie, Richard Church and John Moore. (Cheltenham Library Local Studies Collection)

results were so negligible that he returned half his fee) for the first time.

That year's festival competition purposely selected TV as a medium in preference to stage or radio plays. 'A chance for new writers – Television Play Competition' ran the advertisement. One thousand entries came in and two of the winning plays were televised by the BBC the following year.

Six young writers attended the festival as artists-in-residence, available for panels and chats in the Festival Club. This was an idea put forward by Henriques, who was also responsible for an underlying theme for the festival, originally conceived as the 'Unknown and Little Known in English Literature' but in actuality much more about the mechanics of writing and language. It was not the sort of stuff calculated to attract the general public, and he knew it. He was still irked by their failure of the previous year: 'As the result of not having an independent trust, and so having to depend almost entirely on local audiences, we have to seek for subjects and attractive titles which fetch people out of the streets . . . we have this constant pull of providing popular entertainment on the one hand and providing a serious platform for writers on the other.'

One such event was billed 'An Informal Occasion'. It was organised by the newly formed Cheltenham Literary Festival Society and was presented as an opportunity for the public to meet the writers and other guests over tea. Each of twelve tables would be presided over by one or more celebrity, among them an agent, a bookseller and a publisher. After a set time they would move to another table like a literary version of musical chairs. 'The experiment was apparently too daring for Cheltenham, for the audience presented the most pathetically empty appearance yet seen at a Literary Festival', the *Echo*'s reviewer said of another Young Writers event, chaired by Compton Mackenzie. The festival had made its first serious loss – £450 against guarantees from the Corporation and Arts Council of only £350.

Was it because it was too innovatory? Anti-populist? In fact it fulfilled many of the ideals long articulated in the festival handbook. There were real opportunities for the audience to participate, it featured new as well as established writers, a competition for first-time writers, and for schools there was 'Reading is a Dangerous Drug', a debate between local under-eighteens and festival faithfuls Eric Linklater, Marghanita Laski and Gilbert Harding. And for the crowds there was still the Brains Trust.

There were problems behind the scenes. Valuable time had been wasted in haggling over the trust. The formation of the Festival Society and Council had taken up more time. The judging of the TV play competition was an enormous task. By June the programme still had gaping holes. George Wilkinson had gone on holiday in July (to holiday or not to holiday after the Music Festival is a perennial dilemma of Town Hall staff, exhausted by one festival and immediately under pressure to get on to the next), leaving the handbook for Robert to pick up. The caterers at the Town Hall failed them again, and John rang round hotels and cafés frantic to ensure that the Young Writers dined adequately.

Three days after the festival Robert Henriques sent in his letter of resignation. John Moore was appalled. He had hoped that he would be the one to bow out, or at least they would do so together. Words were exchanged, the last – alliterative – were John's: 'I consider you to have been precipitate, whereas you think me to be pusillanimous and procrastinating, none of these adjectives being stronger than our friendship [which] will survive!'

John Moore directed the 1956 festival on his own. As proof that there were no hard feelings, Robert Henriques chaired the Brains Trust. Then John resigned too.

Why did the Arts Council change their minds? Was it change of policy, a turn in the direction of partnership with local authorities? Were they worried that Cheltenham would bow out, leaving them the festival's only funding body? Or did they think that it would prosper better through local support?

What would have happened if the festival had gone independent in 1955? Would it have thrived and grown? Would it have achieved national and international status sooner, becoming an English Edinburgh? Or would it have disappeared?

As it was the die was cast. The steps were choreographed. From now on the dance would vary in size, in where it took place, in the faces and the length of the haircuts, but it would remain in Cheltenham, a hybrid belonging to both the Council and Cheltenham Arts Festivals, a local event that depended on popular support, which intermittently and then decisively reached out to national and international audiences.

5 SCULPTURES BEWILDERED THE MAYOR

Since the end of the war 'contemporary' has been the word: both the Music and the Literature Festivals have it in their titles and in 1955 they were joined by a newcomer, the Cheltenham Contemporary Art Festival. Taking place in May the inaugural exhibitions – British 'artists of promise as well as fame' organised by the Arts Council and twentieth-century sculpture lent by the Victoria & Albert Museum – attracted over 1000 visitors a day. If the first Art Festival was a success, the second galvanised the town. Contemporary art was to be found everywhere, celebrated in exhibitions, talks, films, workshops and shop displays.

It was a wind of change that transformed the Literature Festival, as a glance at the publicity will show: Cheltenham Festival of Art and Literature 23 September–4 October 1957. Yes, the two festivals have lost their adjective and been rolled into one. A.G. Fletcher, the new curator of Cheltenham Art Gallery, Museum and Library, who started the Contemporary Art Festival, has been co-opted on to the Committee and is presumably responsible for the art side of the festival. As for the literature side, George Wilkinson was probably the one to field and implement suggestions, for the new chairman, A.L. Morris, also the Chair of the Board of Directors, was not a literary man. Rather he represents the consolidation of the Council's control over the festival. One cannot help but ask if John Moore would have welcomed the fusion of the two had he been in the chair. Was it a good idea, or a money-saving piece of bureaucratic tidying? After all, exhibitions with free admission do not generate income. A prevailing opinion seems to have been that artists were not good at talking, so the literary types could provide the majority of the spoken events, leaving the artists to exhibitions and workshops.

With two festivals added together, the programme now took up ten instead of five days. Out of thirteen (instead of eight) events, two were dedicated to art, the remainder a familiar mix including a schools event, a debate between the Oxford and Cambridge Unions, and the Brains Trust. Literary speakers included Rebecca West, H.D. Kitto and Margaret Irwin. The first speaker on art was an ironic choice for a town that counts GCHQ as among its biggest employers – but time had yet to prove him a spy. Sir Anthony Blunt gave a lecture on Picasso, in particular *Guernica*, that near-monotone masterpiece of protest against war.

It was not the Surveyor of the Queen's Pictures who caused consternation in Cheltenham. It was the sculpture exhibition in the gardens behind the Town Hall. 'Sculptures bewildered the Mayor' ran the headline in the *Echo*. 'I suppose that there must be many of us who do not really understand contemporary music or art', he said ingenuously in his introduction to 'The Artist's Conscience and the Public Appetite', the opening address of the Festival given by Sir George Barnes, then Director of Television at the BBC. 'Monstrosities', 'nasty nightmare improbabilities', 'fantastic phantoms', spluttered the letters page in the paper, one signed by 'Anti-humbug'.

What were these abominations? Well, Henry Moore's *King and Queen*, originally promised for 1955 but held up by a flawed casting, had arrived at last. And the rest of the perpetrators are almost all names we still know, among them Barbara Hepworth, Reg Butler, Anthony Caro, Philip King, and Lynn Chadwick. The gardens were floodlit, a 24-hour guard was mounted, and at the end a sculpture called *Meditation* by Willi Soukop was bought by public subscription, a sort of vindication.

The following year the festival eschewed sculpture and the one after it favoured small works (many by the same artists who had shown in the gardens) under the title 'Sculpture in the Home'. It was put on in the safety of the Art Gallery & Museum alongside a selection of work by *Six Young Painters*, the third such exhibition to be arranged for the festival by the Arts Council. From 1956 to 1960 these innovatory shows included artists such as Peter Lanyon, Josef Herman, Michael Andrews, John Bratby, Jack Smith and Edward Middleditch.

The Contemporary Art Society supplied a couple of theme exhibitions; the first called *The Seasons*, the second in 1958 *The Religious Theme*. Although the titles might suggest orthodoxy, both were resolutely modern, their catalogues the acme of the latest in graphic design, and this their first showing after the Tate Gallery in London. Mr Fletcher invited the Bishop of Gloucester to open *The Religious Theme*. The bishop agreed on condition that he did not have to make any bones about his ignorance of contemporary art. This may have prompted Mr Fletcher to ask John Berger, at that time living nearby in Coleford, to come and explain both this exhibition and *Three Masters of Modern Painting* – Sir Matthew Smith, Victor Pasmore and Francis Bacon – in a lecture at the Art Gallery.

Berger's talk was packed, a good reason for his appointment as one of the leaders for the artists' workshops which had started in 1958. The idea was that practising artists would demonstrate and discuss the techniques and basis of study behind contemporary art as distinct from traditional art. That first year Victor Pasmore and Harry Thubron were in charge, with Hubert Dalwood and Kenneth Martin among the Guest Artists. In 1960 the guests were Peter Lanyon, Jeffrey Camp, Sheila Fell and Josef Herman, all of them artists of repute. The idea rubbed off on the literary side as well; workshops led by the 'Guest Writers' (no longer called Young Writers) on 'The Practical Aspects of the Writer's Craft' were held in 1958 and '60.

Henry Moore's *King and Queen* illustrates the cover of the catalogue for the 1957 exhibition. (Courtesy of Cheltenham Art Gallery & Museum)

Art films were always a part of the proceedings, shown sometimes in the Town Hall and sometimes in the Montpellier Rotunda. An hour and a half's viewing would include three or four brief documentaries on a catholic selection of topics. A full-length film *The Picasso Mystery* by Henri-Georges Clouzot was shown at the Daffodil Cinema at 9 o'clock on the two Sunday evenings of the 1958 festival.

Literature Festival *aficionados* tend not to recall much about the exhibitions and art activities, yet they must have done a lot to bring the festival out into the town. Indeed in 1959 even the festival talks were weighted towards art rather than literature because the second week had to be called off for the General Election (polling always takes place in the Town Hall; the possibility of an election at festival time is still a spectre that haunts the organisers). The Guest Writers were cancelled, as were talks by Sir Kenneth Clark, John Wain and Eric Linklater. Although Sir Harold Nicolson gave the opening address, the painter Sir Stanley Spencer was undoubtedly the star of that year, disarming his audience by his simple proclamations, his hopeless pile of notes and his square-cut thatch of hair.

The Foyle's lunches, started in 1953, continued to take place annually. Of all of them, 1958 is the year I would most like to have been there. Paul Robeson and the ballerina Beryl Grey were the unlikely guests. Robeson sang a funeral spiritual and phrases from Mussorgsky's *Boris Godunov*, declaimed Shakespeare and finished up by reciting a poem by Pablo Neruda. But 1956 is the year I would not have wanted to be there. Nicholas Monsarrat, author of the bestseller *The Cruel Sea*, failed to show up for it or his sell-out lecture that evening, letting them know a couple of days later that he had lost his voice and had been ordered by the doctors to stay where he was – in Claridges – an expensive fate, as John Moore pointed out in his 'forgiving letter' (Monsarrat's words).

By 1957, the first of the Art and Literature Festivals, the Literary Festival Society was in its third year, presided over by Noel Newman, a most pleasant man and an ideal chairman, who had a gift for getting things done with the gentlest of urging. During the year the Society organised social and literary events – for example, they hired the Rotunda to see the broadcast of the 1955 prizewinning TV plays. This was the first year of the 'Wine and Cheese Parties', a replacement for the 'Informal Occasion', and destined to become a perennial. A meeting of the festival's National Council usually took place during its course, bringing representatives from the Publishers and Booksellers' Associations, the Royal Society of Literature, PEN, the National Book League, the British Film Institute, the Arts Council and Oxford University to Cheltenham.

The Society now took complete responsibility for hosting the Guest Writers by paying their fees, putting them up and generally entertaining them. Elizabeth Browning was among the most hospitable. She remembers how nervous some members were at the prospect of hosting John Braine, author of *Room at the Top*, and their relief when she offered to put him up. Picnics in the Cotswolds, visits to Tewkesbury Abbey or the Roman Villa at Chedworth were all on the menu. With writers packed into the back of her Bedford

An illustration from the handbook showing Heather and Noel Newman, Jacquetta Hawkes, Lucile and John Moore and J.B. Priestley at the 1955 festival.

van Elizabeth would take off into the glorious autumn countryside in weather which looking back always seemed to be sunny. Vividly remembered by several people is the visit of the actress Mai Zetterling who was newly married to David Hughes, a Guest Writer in 1958. 'She was so glamorous and beautiful, we were all quite transfixed', says Noel Newman's widow, Heather.

Newman was just one of several local businessmen actively involved in the cultural life of the town around this time. Cheltenham has long endured the reputation of being populated largely by retired colonels and the remnants of the British Raj. In fact a far greater number of Cheltonians were employed in the various light industries that had quietly grown up on the outskirts of the town, many of them with a boost from the war. Sir George Dowty of Dowty Aerospace, Richard Walker of Walker Crosweller and Lionel Northcroft of Spirax-Sarco were among those to respond vigorously to save the Pittville Pump Room and the Opera House when they were threatened. The campaign for the Opera House was spearheaded by Derek Malcolm, then on the *Echo* and later of the *Guardian*, and others including Margaret Davies of the Ellenborough Hotel. Noel Newman was roped in to chair an interminable number of meetings, and they succeeding in getting the theatre refurbished to reopen in 1960 as the Everyman Theatre. The festival held another open-air sculpture exhibition that year and chose the gardens around the Pump Room for its location, perhaps a gesture of support for its future.

By 1960, however, things were financially shaky. In 1958 John Moore must have written to almost every writer he could think of asking them to help 'pull the festival out of the red' by donating a signed book or an orginal manuscript to sell at a fundraising bazaar. Attendances at the 1960 festival were down despite an impressive line-up which included Sir Kenneth Clark, a debate on the future of drama between William Douglas-Home and Arnold Wesker, Stephen Potter on 'Gamesmanship in Literature', Nikolaus Pevsner, John Wain, C. Day Lewis, Eric Linklater and 'Controversy', a new-look Brains Trust including Pamela Frankau and Olivia Manning. What did this augur?

6 FIREWORKS!

The 1961 Festival did not take place.

A letter from John Moore to Nicholas Monsarrat gives the explanation: 'When George Wilkinson, the Festival Organiser, sent you that cable in my name he was in a great state of alarm because the whole of the programme was crumbling about him, and no less than 4 of our chief speakers, for various reasons, have at the last moment cried off. He was very relieved to get your cable; but when we sat down to consider what could be done about the rest of the programme, we most regretfully came to the conclusion that there simply wasn't time to put on a Festival which would have been other than makeshift, and that would have done us no good at all.' He was writing on 2 August, by which time they must have been very worried about getting the publicity out in time to advertise the festival adequately, let alone rescue the line-up. It had already been decided that an Art Week would be run separately, and now they were forced to let what was once again the Festival of Contemporary Literature 'lapse' altogether 'for this one year'.

One aspect of it had gone ahead anyway: the fifth Guinness Poetry Competition, which had been held at Cheltenham since 1957. The first prize was awarded to Sylvia Plath for her poem 'Insomniac'. Had the festival taken place, she would have been expected to come to Cheltenham to get her prize. As it was she agreed to be one of the judges for the next year's crop of submissions – 339 of them, fewer than earlier competitions which had attracted over double that number.

The 1961 hiatus was perhaps not a bad thing. In retrospect it may have given the festival time to reinvent itself and burst back on the scene, bigger and better than before. It may also have bolstered the determination of its supporters to see it survive.

Evidence for this lies in the series of three events held by the Festival Society in the early part of 1962 to raise funds. Sonia and Tom Rolt – the L.T.C. Rolt of canal and railway fame, an engineer, writer and before-his-time champion of the industrial past – were the creators of 'Victoriana, a Nineteenth Century Evocation in Sound and Vision', performed at the Pittville Pump Room on 29 March. The Pump Room with its circular gallery above cruciform assembly rooms is, for all its beauty, a challenging space for a performance, but the Rolts were determined to make the most of it. The lights dimmed to the sound of a jet

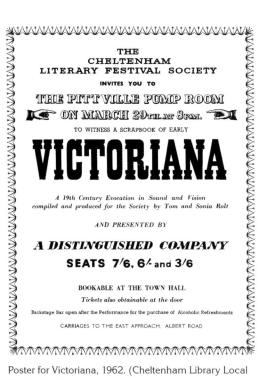

THE
CHELTENHAM
LITERARY FESTIVAL SOCIETY

INVITES YOU TO

THE PITTVILLE PUMP ROOM

ON MARCH 29TH. AT 8P.M.

TO WITNESS A SCRAPBOOK OF EARLY

VICTORIANA

*A 19th Century Evocation in Sound and Vision
compiled and produced for the Society by Tom and Sonia Rolt*

AND PRESENTED BY

A DISTINGUISHED COMPANY

SEATS 7/6, 6/- and 3/6

BOOKABLE AT THE TOWN HALL
Tickets also obtainable at the door

Backstage Bar open after the Performance for the purchase of Alcoholic Refreshments

CARRIAGES TO THE EAST APPROACH. ALBERT ROAD

Poster for Victoriana, 1962. (Cheltenham Library Local Studies Collection)

plane. It faded and was replaced by the distinctive notes of a barrel organ (real). The gallery became an emigration ship with ropes dropped overboard to splash on to the stage below. A Victorian miss read Fanny Burney against a backdrop of lantern slides, a street urchin quoted from Mayhew. It was a hard-earned triumph and the Society followed it with a 'Scrapbook of the Regency' and John Moore's eulogy to olde England, 'The Elizabethans', this time at the Everyman.

But there was another reason for the excitement in the air, the new Honorary Director. Elizabeth Jane Howard had attended the 1956 festival as one of the resident Young Writers shortly after the publication of her second novel, *The Long View*, which was a Book Society Choice and an immediate success. Despite nerves, she had gamely agreed to do three events, including taking up the cudgels against C. Day Lewis in a debate for schools. She and Gillian Freeman, another of the Young Writers, stayed with the Brownings. She saw the Rolts, whom she knew from when she had done secretarial work for the Inland Waterways Association. She thoroughly enjoyed herself and in thanking John Moore offered, 'Do you want ideas for next or future years? All festivals fascinate me and naturally a festival concentrating upon literature is the most interesting of all.'

John must have remembered her interest for it was he who invited her to an interview at the Arts Council in London. She was full of ideas. First of all, it would say 'festival' through and through. It would be international, far-ranging, up-to-date, broad-minded and entertaining. It would have quality, be alive, and appeal to all sorts of readers including children and young adults. . . .

They could have a literary zoo in the gardens – they could borrow an Eeyore, a Peter Rabbit or even a Tigger for the week. The last night could be a wonderful celebration at the Pump Room: song, verse, dancing, champagne and lots of prizes, and finish off with fireworks over the lake. An exhibition of portraits of living writers at the Art Gallery. Recorded messages from great writers of the world could greet festival-goers at the first event.

But did she understand that this would be expensive? OK, well . . . She was sure she could raise the money. Perhaps the newly launched *Sunday Telegraph* might be

Edna O'Brien with Elizabeth Jane Howard and John Moore, 1962. (Courtesy of the *Gloucestershire Echo*)

interested in sponsoring a day? Could they not find someone with in-house publications who could produce the handbook for them? Perhaps another auction of manuscripts could be held on the last night. She could probably persuade quite a lot of her friends to come down for free. As long as they had a marvellous time. There was one thing though: she could not afford to do it without being paid and she would need secretarial help.

By 1962 Jane, as she is called by her friends, was a regular on TV panel shows. As well as the novels, she was writing for *Queen* magazine. She had friends and contacts among writers, artists and the media, and was willing to use them for the festival's benefit.

As for her Cheltenham friends, as Sonia Rolt put it, 'we were absolutely behind her, we ran about hard for her'. Elizabeth Browning, who was now on the Management Committee, put her up when she came down for meetings. John Moore was ready with advice, got a grant for the Guest Writers out of the Society of Authors, and asked his friends for donations for the auction.

Elizabeth Jane Howard was not so impressed by the support offered by officialdom, who often seemed to her keener to get in the way than to help. The exhibition looked as though it would be expensive – insurance, collecting the works. There was no money in the budget. Could they make an entry charge? This would have to go to the Borough

Council for approval. Instead of the usual book exhibition, why not *sell* books, have a sort of book supermarket? It turned out to be a tricky negotiation with the Booksellers Association. At one point it was reported on the radio that she had resigned out of frustration – erroneous, but there was a grain of truth there.

Howard's ideas were ambitious and took an immense amount of work to realise. Hundreds of letters went out – some to request the loan of portraits, some to gather in messages for the opening event, some to request books or manuscripts for the auction, some invitations to speakers. The letters must have been good because the responses are so warm. Eric Linklater applauded: 'Should you choose to abandon the upper levels of literary practice, you will easily earn a living writing begging letters.' Henry Green's refusal is funny in its frankness: 'I am afraid I can't do what you ask. The trouble is that one gives

a manuscript as I did to the Anti Capital Punishment people, it is bought quite cheap, and then sold by the purchaser at about 100% profit. . . . In any case I know you quite well enough to say that I don't care much about the Cheltenham Festival in any case. I was brought up within 9 miles of that town and know how awful it really is. Sorry to be so uncooperative.'

There were letters from E.M. Forster, Richard Hughes, Ivy Compton Burnett, Agatha Christie, Elizabeth Bowen and Leonard Woolf – writers who for one reason or another would never appear at the festival, but might have contributed from afar. William Gerhardi was among those who recorded a question for the Brains Trust on the opening night. Herman Hesse agreed too, but died before he could do so.

A drawing of E.M. Forster by Sir John Rothenstein shown in the 'Portraits of Living Writers' exhibition, 1962. (Courtesy of the Provost and Fellows of King's College, Cambridge)

'The amount of work was colossal. It took eight months out of my working life', said Jane, and the director's fee of £300, large perhaps for the Cheltenham budget, she found too small to live on in London.

The handbook was produced by Schweppes, possibly due to John Moore's Savile Club connections with the chairman and Stephen Potter, who was responsible for the sophisticate copy of their ads:

Plural: *Schweppës Schweppës Schweppsum*
The *noun* I decline, but the *drinks* I accepsum

It was packed with advertisements and a festival programme which promised more speakers than ever before: nine Guest Writers including Edna O'Brien and Lynne Reid Banks, a ten-person panel for the opening Brains Trust, three major discussion events, four talks and the Grand Finale.

The exhibition *Portraits of Living Writers* was opened on the Saturday afternoon before the festival by Peter Scott, Elizabeth Jane Howard's first husband. It was an impressive assembly of paintings, sculpture and drawings, most of them borrowed from private collections – Somerset Maugham by Marie Laurencin and Graham Sutherland, Henry Green by Matthew Smith, T.S. Eliot by Epstein and Patrick Heron, Aldous Huxley by Vanessa Bell, and Evelyn Waugh and Anthony Powell by Henry Lamb. Jane was furious that the chairman and his Board did not make an appearance and said so to the local newspaper. The low attendance may have had something to do with the weather. Outside a stupendous gale was brewing up. That night the wind uprooted forty-two trees and whipped a temporary roof off the Municipal Offices in the Promenade.

Jane had rented a house in St George's Road near the Town Hall so that she could host the writers herself with the help of a housekeeper. 'It meant they could have sandwiches at midnight, or come back for a kip in the middle of the day and have the choice of privacy or chat.'

There were many memorable events that week. The historian Cecil Woodham-Smith's talk entitled 'The Papers in the Attic' made a lasting impression – she was completely unpretentious about her skills, highly intelligent and exquisitely turned out. A discussion about the theatre between Peter Shaffer, John Mortimer and Gwyn Thomas, an entertaining and voluble Welshman, was 'instantly so intense that we were enthralled. They were oblivious of the audience, so it felt as if one was eavesdropping and no-one wanted to interrupt in case they stopped.'

Peregrine Worsthorne arrived ten minutes late for a discussion titled 'Newspapers', having driven flat out from the Labour conference in Brighton. The *Sunday Telegraph*, for which he worked, had indeed sponsored a whole day – a first for the Literature Festival – which allowed Elizabeth Jane Howard to bring Carson McCullers and Joseph Heller from the States, and Romain Gary from France to speak in a symposium on 'Sex in Literature' (a reminder that 1963 was the year of the *Lady Chatterley's Lover* trial).

The other member of the team was Kingsley Amis. 'He was the only writer whom I did not personally invite', said Jane. 'The *Sunday Telegraph* announced they had done so without consulting me. I then wrote the formal letter.' They had met a couple of times in passing when they had appeared on the same television programmes.

The event was not altogether easy. Carson McCullers was ill and in pain. Jane had had to find her a full-time nurse so that she could be at the festival at all. Carson's speech was so blurry that Jane had to repeat all that she said. The best moment was probably Joseph Heller's comment on censorship: 'I think a line does have to be drawn, but I don't

Kingsley Amis. (*Observer*/Godfrey MacDomnic)

know anyone I'd trust to draw it.' This brought an acknowledging nod from Amis, who had also endorsed Carson McCullers's assertion that Jane Austen's books were pornographic: 'Yes, I see what you mean – it's a sort of pecuniary pornography.'

Afterwards there was the usual move to the bar, and that night Kingsley and Jane found themselves staying up to talk, long after everyone had gone to bed. This was the prelude to the love affair followed by the marriage that was to make them for many years the most celebrated literary couple in London.

One suspects that everyone fell in love with Jane that festival. She was beautiful and lovely to watch, warm and clever and charming. Laurie Lee came to the festival as an old friend of hers, writing beforehand, 'I think you must be the best Artistic Director Chelt. ever had, and I'm glad my first appearance here would be looped to your beautiful skirts'; and afterwards, '*You* should be thanked, for the miracle you worked. The whole of Cheltenham should be driven out in the streets and made to cry "Ta!" in one great shout.' He went to the Grand Finale, was forced on stage as part of the writers' entertainment, and loved it all. In particular he thought 'The fireworks were dazzlers – some of the best I've seen in this country, partly due to the exquisite setting which lit up those great park trees both from without and within until they became fireworks too.' He finished, 'I hope you'll do it again'.

This was the hope of the Board and the Management Committee and most of all of John Moore, who quite sincerely wanted to pass on the baton. He agreed to do the 1963 festival, and made sure it was a worthy successor to 1962, but the understanding was that there was still hope that Elizabeth Jane Howard would do 1964. She didn't. No one did.

7 NARROW TIES AND DARK SUITS

The lack of a festival in 1964 was an indication of the predicament in which Cheltenham Arts Festivals found themselves. The 1963 Music Festival had made a substantial loss. Elizabeth Jane Howard had been the first Artistic Director they had ever paid, and she had not found it enough. The auction on the last night had raised over £700, but this does not seem to have rescued the festival's finances enough to boost the Director's fee.

The Literary Festival Society had been disbanded in 1963, perhaps because Noel Newman was fully occupied as chair of the Everyman Theatre (which had almost gone under because the formidably snowy winter of 1962/3 prevented audiences getting into town). The festival's National Council, on the other hand, was resuscitated to help resolve the difficulties over a director. Publisher John Calder, novelist Gabriel Fielding (one of the recommendations for the 1954 First Novel Competition), poet Patric Dickinson and several others were tried, but it was not until the autumn of 1964 that the Committee interviewed Ian Hamilton, a young poet not long out of Oxford. He edited a literary magazine called *The Review*, and had been suggested by Committee member Alan Hancox, who used to buy letters and autograph manuscripts from him as a way of supporting the magazine.

In retrospect Ian Hamilton thinks that the Committee did not know which way to turn once Elizabeth Jane Howard had dropped out of the picture. Should they continue to broaden their horizons, or keep it local? Ian's appointment as 1965 director was a vote for the former. He likes to claim that they appointed him because while he knew what was going on in the metropolitan world of literature, he was young enough to be fairly obedient, and perhaps – not said, but one wonders – less exacting about a fee.

The first event of the 1965 festival was a discussion titled 'Pop Culture', a clear appeal to a new generation. If the panel were more culture than pop, in the sense of the Beatles and teenage discos at the Town Hall, it was a mix of a kind not seen at Cheltenham before. Jazz was represented by George Melly and folk by Ewan MacColl, Christopher Ricks and Richard Hoggart were the unstuffy academics, and the team was completed by Jonathan Miller, billed as an original member of *Beyond the Fringe*. The talk got a little intense so George Melly, a bit left out at the far end of the table and bored, started a silent and elaborate conversation with a neighbouring dahlia, part of the floral decorations, causing outbursts of hilarity among the audience.

After the interval Ewan MacColl joined Peggy Seeger and other folk musicians for a recital introduced by Alasdair Clayre, author, song-writer and Fellow of All Souls. Led by Clayre who stayed the week, folk music was to pop up throughout the rest of the proceedings, mostly late night at the Festival Club and particularly if another act had not showed up. Singer Frankie Armstrong was a surprise guest one such night.

Every day offered a full evening's worth in two parts: usually a discussion followed by some different form of entertainment. The second day John McGahern, David Storey and Gabriel Fielding took apart 'Character in the Modern Novel', and after the break Al Alvarez introduced readings by some of the poets he had included in *The New Poetry* – John Fuller, Michael Hamburger, Geoffrey Hill with the addition of Guest Writer Hugo Williams (twenty-three and in a state of anticipation, having postponed his wedding in Paris to take part).

Ian Hamilton was a little disappointed that the hall was not fuller for the two evenings which he had specially hoped would appeal to the crowds: one on crime and literature, the other on sci-fi. The panels were impressive: the former included Patricia Highsmith, Julian Symons and H.R.F. Keating, the latter Anthony Burgess and Brian Aldiss. Hamilton came to the conclusion that readers of popular genre fiction were not necessarily the kind of people to sit around and talk about books. Nevertheless the crime evening ended on a popular note with a packed showing of the film of J.M. Synge's *The Playboy of the Western World* at the Daffodil Cinema, to this day remembered as a rare instance of late-night film in Cheltenham.

On the last night Charles Causley, Gavin Ewart and Stevie Smith, who could be wonderfully funny in front of an audience, provided the writers' entertainment. The Cheltenham Prize, started by Elizabeth Jane Howard and given by an anonymous donor, was awarded for the third and last year, so too were the Guinness Poetry Prizes, and there was an auction of books and manuscripts. It was similar to the Grand Finale of 1963, but this time it was folk song that went with the cabaret.

A drama evolved through the week. Hamilton had invited two East German poets, Günter Kunert and Manfred Bieler, whom he had recently featured in his magazine. Visas were successfully negotiated for them, not an easy thing at that time; they were to arrive on a Polish flight from East Berlin. As time drew on the festival was disappointed to hear that they would not be coming after all as their visas were in West Berlin and they could not collect them without – yes – visas. Two days before the start, a telegram arrived. They *had* their visas, they *would* be coming to speak as scheduled on the Tuesday. On Monday there was another telegram. Their government had refused permission for them to leave. On Tuesday evening Alasdair Clayre performed in their place at the Festival Club. But

Ian Hamilton (in dark glasses) leaving *The New Review* offices in Soho. (Hugo Williams, via Cargo Press)

eventually they turned up and, as the paper put it, 'made history' by appearing with West German poet Erich Fried at Friday's Festival Club. One forgets what rare birds they must have been at the time: what struck people was how different the East Germans were from each other – the one ascetic and idealistic, the other worldly and westernised.

Ian Hamilton had continued the practice of Guest Writers, but in the absence of the Festival Society their fees were now funded by their publishers. The poet Alan Brownjohn, who was one of the team in 1967, points out that those were the days when poetry was selling astonishingly well and publishers were consequently prepared to spend money. He looks back on his visit as 'a week with companions one liked, with a dash of absurdity and glamour thrown in', as well as the serious business of wordmongering.

The Guest Writers were put up at the George Hotel in St George's Road, close to the Town Hall. The first evening of the festival everyone would be invited to meet in the bar for drinks, then they would have dinner together before moving on to the Town Hall. Ian says 'The George was crucial, everybody stayed there. There was a lot of drinking. After dinner two taxis would take the evening's dignitaries to the Town Hall and the rest would get a lift or follow on foot. There was an old Polish night porter whose life was made a misery by the comings and goings of writers at two in the morning.'

The speakers would be collected by George Wilkinson who regarded his director – if Ian is to be believed – as 'not much good at all the bureaucracy stuff. He was efficient and long-suffering. I was always late with everything – for example, proofs that had to go to press, or I'd be found in the bar talking to the writers when they were late to go on stage. I think George thought we were all amateurish, and didn't know how the real world ran.' Alan Brownjohn demurs: 'Ian's organisation was extremely efficient – after all he got all those people there. After dinner, he would say quietly "OK, guys, let's go" and one did. He had authority and masses of charisma.'

In 1966 the Guest Writers revolted. Insurrection was in the air from the beginning when in the closing moments of the opening event (attended by the mayor as usual), a discussion on 'The Anatomy of Publishing', the panel was interrupted by one of the Guest Writers accusing its members of talking 'codswallop'. Charles Osborne, Literature Director of the Arts Council, had announced new bursaries for writers. A panellist had responded by saying that the Arts Council should not be 'an extended arm of National Assistance'. The infuriated heckler was protesting on behalf of poorer writers 'who lived on beans and toast'.

The next occasion was the Foyle's lunch which took place on the same day as a discussion titled 'The Feminine Sensibility' with Brigid Brophy and the women Guest Writers – Margaret Drabble, Maureen Duffy and Laura Del Rivo. Brigid Brophy was seated next to the guest of honour, Malcolm Muggeridge, at the Foyle's lunch, but none of the Guest Writers was invited and neither was the festival director. Under the newspaper photograph of the evening panel (who had by and large agreed that feminine sensibility was a myth) dressed in miniskirts and trousers ran the line 'We were snubbed'.

The previous night's event was by all accounts one of the festival's greats. It was a tribute to Samuel Beckett and consisted of a talk by Christopher Ricks illustrated with readings by Patrick Magee – Beckett's favourite actor at the time – and Harold Pinter.

Later in the week a frail Edmund Blunden, only recently installed as Professor of Poetry at Oxford, recounted his 'Literary Recollections', and a panel of leading playwrights including Edward Bond, Frank Marcus – best remembered for *The Killing of Sister George* – and David Storey discussed contemporary drama, with John Willett, authority on Brecht and a colleague of Hamilton, who now worked for the *Times Literary Supplement*, in the chair.

Margaret Drabble. (Mark Gerson)

On the last night first prize in the Guinness Poetry Competition went to Monica J.F. Ditmass, a teacher at Cheltenham Ladies' College. Second prize was awarded to 'Seamus Heaney of Belfast', for his poem 'The Outlaw'.

Alan Brownjohn, poet Anthony Thwaite, writer and critic Derwent May, and authors Eva Figes (not yet identified as feminist), Shena MacKay, Gillian Tindall and Gillian Freeman constituted the 1967 Guest Writers. Ian Hamilton remembers that 'everyone fell in love with Shena Mackay. One notably uptight poet threw himself into a holly bush with excitement. I suppose he was trying to impress her and wanted to seem a party animal . . . '. Richard Boston, then a colleague at the *TLS*, agrees: 'she was very pretty as well as being a good writer. She was shy and had a very soft voice, so one felt one had to protect her.'

Boston wrote an article about the festival for the *New York Times Book Review*. He described leading authors playing conkers at midnight in the street (the paper added a

CHELTENHAM FESTIVAL OF LITERATURE

SATURDAY, 7th October

at the Pittville Pump Room
at 8 p.m.

_____

WINE AND CHEESE PARTY

AWARD OF THE GUINNESS POETRY PRIZES

Reading of the entries for the Guinness Poetry Competition and award of prizes by Lord Moyne

A LITERARY ENTERTAINMENT

JOAN GREENWOOD
RHONDDA GILLESPIE
ANDRE MORELL
Introduced by Denby Richards

Joan Greenwood and Rhondda Gillespie in a dramatic recitation "The Mournful Monk", by Liszt, setting of a poem by Lenau for narrator and piano (translation by William Mann).

Liszt: Petrarch Sonnet No. 123
Rhondda Gillespie, preceded by a reading of the Sonnet by Andre Morell.

Literary readings by Joan Greenwood and Andre Morell.

Ticket 10/-

The finale of the 1967 festival (and the occasion of Seamus Heaney's first visit to Cheltenham).

succinct outline of the rules for American readers) and letting off fireworks from hotel windows. He said that Stephen Spender's lecture, which compared English and American poetry, was the 'solidest contribution' to the festival, but he was more amused by the opening event on the 'Comic Novel' which, because of faulty microphones, attained 'an air of farce normally lacking in discussions of comedy'. William Trevor, Michael Frayn, Shena MacKay and Gillian Tindall struggled to to be understood. Inaudibility was a refuge for the chairman, who mumbled to disguise the fact he did not know what books they had written. Anthony Burgess did not arrive, although he was expected. Meanwhile, speaking at the Foyle's lunch, Barbara Cartland inveighed against 'Swinging London', so-called intellectuals and the 'avalanche of dirt and filth that has come over our country'.

Ian Hamilton's three festivals were fun, full of poets, tended to veer towards the intellectual, and brought a breath of fresh air to Cheltenham.

The sad event of 1967 was the death of John Moore on 27 July, unexpectedly, although cancer had been diagnosed. A dedication in the handbook spoke of the great debt the festival owed him. Robert Henriques also died that year, having battled with the same disease for ten years.

8 FICTIONAL REVOLUTION

Cheltenham 1967 inspired Richard Boston to write a novel called *Amorous Causes*. It is set in a fictitious town called Dalchester. The hotel where the festival guests stay is described in detail: it is called the Queen's and outside – with its columned portico and revolving doors – it resembles the real hotel of that name. The company assembles in the bar and dinner is served: 'a block booking from the Town Hall for four tables. Melon or soup, steak-chips-and-veg, ice cream, fruit salad or cheese.' Wine has not been included, so they order ' the most expensive' from the pretty waitress, 'and put it on Mr Lilley's bill, will you?' Mr Lilley is the director of the festival, 'an ex-military man, fluent, urbane and very smooth, with a crisp manner that suggested that he had everything under control'.

Afterwards they find 'that there were two taxis waiting to go to the meeting. Some people got into them hopefully and then had to get out again because they were being reserved for special people – that is to say the panel and Lilley himself.' In the foyer of the Corn Exchange where the festival takes place 'A school blackboard on an easel announced tonight's attraction. . . . This notice contrasted with the posters on the walls . . . which announced the Corn Exchange's usual entertainments – bingo, roller skating and wrestling'. It is recognisably Cheltenham Town Hall.

Inside the mayor is welcoming audience and speakers to the Dalchester Festival. Then Mr Lilley appears, fusses around with glasses and water jugs and blows into the microphone. The panel, which is there to discuss 'The Novel – Is It Dead?', has not long been on stage before there's a shout from the back: '"Can't hear a word". . . the microphone was having some difficulty in making the adjustment from bingo and wrestling.' As the plot develops the festival speakers wind themselves up into a state of 1968-style revolt and proclaim themselves the Dalchester Free Festival.

In the real world of Cheltenham 1968, however, the necessity for bigger box office was hauling the festival back on to more sober tracks. The Management Committee felt they could dispense with a director if there were others whose contacts and advice were at their disposal. Thus the poet C. Day Lewis and Paul Humphreys, a senior producer for Midland BBC Radio who had been a member of the Committee since he had judged the

Radio Play Competition in 1956, were invited to act as Honorary Advisers to the festival.

C. Day Lewis became Poet Laureate in 1968. His association with Cheltenham dated back to the early 1930s when he taught at the junior school of Cheltenham College. A communist and 'known to have committed poetry' (as he phrased it), he bore the brunt of the headmaster's ready suspicion of anything or anyone unusual and was continually finding himself 'carpeted' – for wearing a green shirt when painting his house, Box Cottage in Charlton Kings, or for publishing the love poems he wrote to his wife. Financial anxiety and a hole in the roof induced him to write a whodunnit which was published under the pseudonym of Nicholas Blake, the first of twenty.

Cecil was the first president of the Cheltenham Literary Society and would send notes to John Moore to exhort him to come to meetings, or approach notables for a literary banquet. Little did they know that in 1949 their roles would be reversed. Day Lewis was a loyal friend and supporter of the festival until his death in 1972. He was a superb reader of verse, but disliked talking on stage: 'I'm simply no hand at all at public discussion', he averred in more than one letter. In 1968 he was busy, not well and living some distance away, so his support of the festival could not amount to much more than goodwill and his name on the letterhead.

This left Paul Humphreys, the Committee and George Wilkinson to formulate the programme and secure the speakers. In 1968 they were helped by a local literary figure,

The Everyman Theatre as it looked in the 1960s and '70s. (Courtesy of the *Gloucestershire Echo*)

the critic and biographer Harry Coombes. A friend of F.R. Leavis and staunch supporter of his views, he paved the way for Paul Humphreys and his wife Eileen to pay a visit to Cambridge. They succeeded in persuading Leavis to open the Festival by delivering an original paper. He took as his subject 'T. S. Eliot and the Life of English Literature', and it was titled the Cheltenham Lecture – thus beginning an unbroken annual tradition of celebrity lectures that has survived thirty-two years to date. Coombes took charge of the Guest Writers that year, chairing informal discussions every evening after the main event. Significant among them were poet, actor and columnist P.J. Kavanagh and playwright Ronald Harwood, both of whom later directed the festival.

The character of that year's festival was affected by the decision to hold it in the Everyman Theatre rather than the Town Hall, probably because of continued complaints about the sound in the Main Hall. Three out of the six evenings were given over to staged events, including Micheal Mac Liammoir in his one-man show *The Importance of Being Oscar* and an entertainment by the Barrow Poets.

The acoustics at the Everyman are excellent. One of the famous Matcham theatres, it was built in 1891, a compact and charming theatre for an audience of about 650 people. Steeply stepped balconies give a sense of intimacy even when one is sitting up in the gods. Space backstage and front of house, particularly before it was revamped in 1983-6, was at a premium, so it is no surprise that book exhibitions became a casualty of the new venue. When the festival returned – in part – to the Town Hall in 1971, the book exhibitions came back too, and were to survive into the 1980s.

With few events, big names and ready-made 'shows', the 1968 festival achieved its pecuniary ends. The next year followed a similar format. Arthur Koestler gave the Cheltenham Lecture, C. Day Lewis the poetry reading, there was a one-man show on the Wordsworth Circle by the poet's great-great grandson, and the Barrow Poets again supplied the light-hearted finale. But the Arts Council, whose support had been unswerving since the hiccough of the mid-fifties, were not satisfied with the content of the programmes, nor the local level of funding, particularly Gloucestershire County Council's contribution. Shortly before the 1970 festival Eric White, who had represented the Arts Council on the Committee since 1956, announced that the £1,000 grant would be cut to £800. Consequently the search was on in earnest for a 1971 director to give it a lift, but in the meantime 1970 was to be the last 'directorless' festival. It was also George Wilkinson's last. He had been Spa and Entertainments Manager since 1932.

In 1969 Ronald Harwood had chaired the Guest Writers' events (Melvyn Bragg, Geoffrey Grigson and Antonia Fraser among them). In 1970 it was Douglas Cleverdon, recently retired from the BBC. In these years, the Guest Writers plus more occasional speakers took over an upper room of the Plough Hotel, an old coaching inn on the High Street near the Everyman. Many people recall the atmosphere of these sessions – the talking late into the night, the intimacy, the rather appealing seen-better-days seediness of their surroundings –

P.J. Kavanagh on the Cotswold Hills. (Laurence Whitfield)

with as much affection as earlier habitués regarded the Festival Club. Subsequent events suggest that the role of chair was given to those the Committee hoped to ease into the bigger task of directing the whole festival, for Douglas was appointed director for 1971 and Harwood, wooed for several years, eventually took on 1975.

Douglas Cleverdon must go down in audio history as the man who produced Dylan Thomas's *Under Milk Wood*, perhaps the most famous radio play ever. Winner of several Italia Prizes and other European and American awards, he brought – pertinent to Cheltenham – the Brains Trust to British radio in 1941. Poets particularly liked working with him, and he counted many among his friends. He loved fine books and published several himself, with illustrations by artists such as Eric Gill, David Jones and John Piper. His widow Nest Cleverdon says that after he retired he was 'fearfully worried in case he was not going to have enough money, so he took on every bit of work that was offered him, which was mostly poetry festivals'. Among others he did the Stratford-upon-Avon Poetry Festival, an annual since 1951 on Sundays through the summer.

The first event of Cleverdon's Cheltenham Festival was called 'Words Words Words', an entertainment devised by George Rylands for the Apollo Society with Judi Dench, Michael Williams and Patrick Garland as readers. George (or Dadie) Rylands and Peggy Ashcroft were the founding members of the society which put on mixed programmes of readings and music (for example at Cheltenham in 1950). Douglas Cleverdon had produced and devised shows for them for many years, and the addition of a stage event on a Sunday (when actors are free of their weekday obligations) occurred to him as a good way to start the Festival. The Cheltenham Lecture was given by Nevill Coghill, from whom Cleverdon had commissioned a series of translations of the *Canterbury Tales* for the BBC's Third Programme. Poetry was represented by a reading of Sylvia Plath's poems by Al Alvarez and Margaret Drabble. Cleverdon, who was close to Ted Hughes and usually made a point

Douglas Cleverdon. (Courtesy of Nest Cleverdon)

of programming poets reading their own work, originally planned it as a Hughes/Plath recital, but clearly this did not work out.

Nest Cleverdon particularly remembers a talk by Robert Gittings, a BBC colleague of her husband's and biographer of John Keats, which used two voices to trace the alterations the poet made in drafting 'The Eve of St Agnes', an idea he and Douglas later developed for radio. 'Douglas had thirty year's experience of producing, and had a highly developed sense of performance', says Nest, important skills to bring to a festival. She also mentions the last-night jamboree, which starred their old friend A.L. Lloyd, singer and expert on world folk song, and a band called the High Level Ranters. 'Our son Lewis was living in a commune in the Cotswolds and he turned up with a bunch of completely dotty-looking hippies, who turned out to be frightfully nice, and we all square-danced like mad in the Pittville Pump Room.' It must be one of the few occasions when exuberance succeeded in overcoming the stiffness generally brought on by all that Regency splendour.

9 THE GREAT SWITCHEROO

On 14 November 1973 a photograph appeared on an inner page of the *Echo*. The caption begins 'After the controversial short story competition during the Cheltenham Literary Festival. . .'. It shows the Secretary-General of the Arts Council, the mayor and his wife, and the editor of the *Daily Telegraph* magazine. 'Programme Director Mr Paul Humphreys' stands in the middle, smiling amiably. Everyone else looks grim, particularly 'Mr F.D. Littlewood, Festival Vice-President, who walked out during Mr Dahl's story'. Then one notices another face looking somewhat amused, only half visible behind the others – Roald Dahl.

In the second year of his directorship, Paul Humphreys held a short story competition, sponsored by the *Telegraph* magazine, which published the winners. It attracted 3,000 entries. Roald Dahl was one of a panel of judges – with Susan Hill, publisher Diana Athill and Humphreys himself – and had been invited to speak about short story writing at the prizegiving. When the night came, Paul Humphreys made his introductions as usual and sat down at one side of the stage. Roald Dahl rose to speak. He told the audience that he did not agree with the prizewinning entries and had 'already had a row with the judges'. Instead of the expected talk, he said he would read one of his own stories. It was due to be published in *Playboy* and was called 'The Great Switcheroo', a tale of wife-swapping. It was soon clear that it included a great deal of explicit sex. Pinned to his chair with embarrassment, Paul Humphreys could see unease rippling through the rows. One or two rose to leave. Then he saw Frank Littlewood, now chair of the Management Committee as well as Vice-president of the Company, stand and make his way emphatically to the exit. Paul Humphreys received several sympathetic letters afterwards. It seems characteristic of him that he should have been the only one smiling in the photograph, for he is a radiantly nice man.

Like Douglas Cleverdon, Humphreys brought his BBC radio contacts and expertise to his festivals in 1972–3. He scripted an event for 1973 on Byron's letters called 'The Uncautious Letter-writer' using Ronald Harwood and Rosalind Shanks as readers. Rosalind Shanks had done programmes for Paul at the BBC and she also appeared at the festival opener, a look at the 'Phenomenon of Englishness' written and presented by Basil Boothroyd.

W.H. Auden gave the Cheltenham Lecture the first year, a coup for Paul, who had heard that he would be returning from America that autumn to live in Oxford as a fellow of All Souls. An early note from New York, written in flimsy handwriting on the thinnest of airmail paper, ends 'P.S. My lecture will be more theological than literary.' It was titled 'Work, Carnival and Prayer'.

By dint of a trip to Paris, Humphreys managed to secure another eminent speaker for the following year, the novelist Maurice Druon, then Minister for Cultural Affairs. However his speech on the 'State as Patron of the Arts' lacked the éclat that Paul had hoped for, perhaps because his accent combined with a heavy cold made it – yes – hard to hear, even though it was held at Cheltenham College rather than the Town Hall.

Less successful was Paul's attempt to secure Philip Larkin, who thanked him for his invitation 'but quite honestly I would rather not get into a situation where I might have to say quite bluntly that this or that living writer is in my opinion no good, and I think this might all too easily arise from the kind of programme you adumbrate'. As consolation he added, 'In fact, as you probably know, I go about very little, so there is no danger of my agreeing to a similar proposal from anyone else'.

The one discussion of contemporary literature in 1972 – 'The Avant Garde, a Discussion of Progressive Trends', featuring Michael Holroyd and Paul Scott among others – was not well attended. Next year he tried Susan Hill, publisher T.G. Rosenthal and P.J. Kavanagh speaking on 'The Business of Literature', chaired by Ronald Harwood.

There is a connection to be made between several elements of Paul Humphreys' second festival. Cheltenham College, the boys' public school, had been involved with the Festival from its inception – in the early days through its headmasters, first A.G. Eliot-Smith, next and more importantly the Revd A.G.G.C. Pentreath, whose advice and support on the Advisory Panel was much valued by Moore and Henriques, then through English masters such as R.E.C. Swann, Kit Browning, and later John (known as Jack) Ralphs. Ralphs, who joined the Committee in 1966, had acted with P.J. Kavanagh (who moved to the Cotswolds in 1964) at Oxford. Kavanagh knew Ronald Harwood from the days when they were both professional actors, and they first appeared at Cheltenham in 1968 as two of the Guest Writers. It was perhaps Jack's influence that allowed the festival in 1973 to use the school's great lecture hall, known as Big Classical, when a mix-up over dates meant they lost the Everyman. Since that first visit Kavanagh and Harwood had become regulars.

In a 1974 press interview P.J. Kavanagh described himself as 'appalled' when he was first approached to

Paul Humphreys.

77. St Mark's Place
New York City,
New York 10003

Feb 11th, 1972

Dear Mr Humphreys:

Thank you for your letter. So far
as I know, Monday Nov 13th is O.K.

yours sincerely

W.H. Auden

P.S. My lecture will be more theological
than literary.

Letter from W.H. Auden to Paul Humphreys, 1972.

direct the festival. One can imagine why for he is a private man, despite a public side to his career as actor, TV presenter, broadcaster and columnist that fitted alongside a more solitary life as poet, writer and countryman. At the time his public profile was especially high, in particular because of a series for BBC TV, *Journey through Summer*. South West Arts, who inherited the funding of the festival from the Arts Council in 1973, had found that although they were proud to harbour 'the only one of its kind in the country' they considered the programme 'too narrow' and were pushing for the broadening influence of a new director.

Kavanagh took up the charge, thoughtfully. In the introduction to the handbook he points out that 'No man sits down to write "literature", no one sits down to read it. We read, and some of us write, books.' His intention is to examine the 'nuts and bolts which hold books together; the use, in other words, of words.' He advocates 'commonsense observation of common things' as the starting point for good writing.

The 1974 festival opened with a tribute to Dr Johnson, 'the tormented apostle of common sense', as Patrick described him, in the form of a revue titled 'The Boswell and Johnson Show' featuring Timothy West and Prunella Scales.

The publicity announced it as the '25th Cheltenham Festival of Literature'. The absence of 1961 and 1964 actually made it the 24th. Kingsley Amis's lecture on G.K. Chesterton was also billed as the '25th Cheltenham Lecture', with less reason as it was only the 7th. This may have been due to an attack of marketing brought on by lack of press coverage the previous year. For the second time the festival boasted a press officer, a member of the Committee called Michael Dineen, and that year a gratifying collection of cuttings from national newspapers testified to his success.

Most of the papers fastened on an event about fiction and journalism featuring Philip Toynbee, Michael Frayn and Auberon Waugh, with Brian Redhead in the chair. James Cameron did not make it. Toynbee, whom Patrick describes as 'not a natty dresser' to the extent that he was only reluctantly allowed into the Town Hall by the doorman, stripped down to a green towelling sweatshirt before attacking Redhead's assertion that writing was like music, an art which should push forward the human predicament: 'that's typical romantic crap' (The Times) or 'this is typical romantic rubbish' (Echo). The writer was not an artist, Toynbee contended, simply a craftsman like a carpenter.

With an Irish great-grandfather, Patrick perhaps had licence to title the final night 'Paddy's Place is Behind the Mixer', featuring four poets – Seamus Heaney, Pearse Hutchinson, Derek Mahon and John Montague – from 'north and south of the troublesome border' who read their work and explored 'the special nature of Irishness'. 'Liberal Irish hospitality' was promised and the night went well, apart from the Pump Room gremlin which tried, once again, to swallow up their words.

Despite an uncertainty about the integrity of a festival dedicated to the essentially solitary occupations of reading and writing, Kavanagh went on to direct the 1976 and 1977 festivals. Before that, however, he succeeded in persuading Ronald Harwood to take on 1975. Actor and writer, a raconteur with an easy friendliness to him, Harwood's appearances at Cheltenham had already endeared him to audiences and the Committee. At that time he was chiefly a novelist and his first big success as a playwright, The Dresser in 1980, was still ahead of him. His interest in theatre disposed him towards a festival that pushed the boundaries towards performed literature rather than discussions of books.

As usual the Sunday night entertainment was a theatrical compilation, this year starring Judi Dench, Leo McKern and Edward Fox in 'Rogues and Vagabonds', a history of actors. Unusually, the final night took place in the lofty, wood-panelled splendour of the Princess Hall in Cheltenham Ladies' College with 'Hail, Horrors, Hail', Christopher Lee's recital of macabre poetry compiled by Charles Osborne, Literature Director of the Arts Council. With his administrative hat on Osborne took part in a symposium on funding for literature. 'Literature isn't the poor relation: it's the beggar', reads a quote in the new-style festival broadsheet from another participant, novelist Maureen Duffy, who tirelessly and successfully spearheaded the Public Lending Right campaign. As a member of the Arts Council Literature Panel, such issues were close to Ronnie's heart for he was and is a great taker-up of causes.

But the big event of the 1975 festival is not to be found in the printed programme. The Russian poet Yevgeny Yevtushenko, at the time a hero in his land with public appearances attracting tens of thousands, came to the festival at the last minute. Ronnie says that getting him over was a matter of 'perilous negotiations'. On his arrival the poet was given a civic welcome by the mayor, and Lord Snow (C.P.) delivered an oration. Yevtushenko then performed his poetry with all the gusto and emotion of the Russian style, interspersed with the English translations read in a more laconic style by P.J. Kavanagh.

Afterwards, the party moved on to the Kavanagh's house, high on a hill in the Cotswolds. The poet swept in, fully the star. 'Sope, sope! I want sope!' Patrick showed him to the bathroom. 'No, no. *Sope!*' Eventually they understood. Kate, Patrick's wife, with the help of the blender and some shepherd's pie, made an enormous bowl of something she hoped bore a resemblance to a hearty Russian soup.

Sadly, the biggest scheduled event of the week, a celebration of Jane Austen written by Paul Bailey and starring, to Harwood's great delight, Celia Johnson, was blighted by the bad acoustics in the Main Hall. 'I stood there in agony. She was superb, but you just could not hear her. Everybody complained and I sympathised with them.' He says that he felt personally to blame. 'Being the Artistic Director was a bit like being a head waiter. Everybody came to you and you felt you had to sort out their table setting.' Exhausted, he went back to London.

If Yevtushenko was the high point of 1975, the poetry competition was the triumph of 1976. Poetry competitions were hardly new to the festival. Bryan Guinness – Lord Moyne – a poet himself, sponsored the Guinness Poetry Prizes from 1957 to 1969 as part of the Cheltenham Festival. On the day of the prizegiving he, or in some years his wife, would arrive in their Rolls to host a luxurious lunch before the evening ceremony. In 1972 a poetry competition was again held, but for some reason – probably the wholehearted support of the *Telegraph* magazine and its editor John Anstey, who offered substantial prizes and publication – the 1976 competition attracted an all-time record number of entries, 21,000 poems in all. Kavanagh says he read them all before sending the 600 best on to the judges . . . 'or at least the first and last lines'! The winners were Charles Tomlinson, George Mackay Brown and Edwin Morgan, all professional poets.

Realising that there was 'a vast reservoir of enthusiasm for poetry' Kavanagh must have persuaded the Committee to allow him to put on a festival largely dedicated to poetry. Dorothy Tutin read Thomas Hardy, Robert Gitting spoke about him. Patrick himself read 'that fine forgotten poet' Ivor Gurney. Five of the fourteen events were readings by living poets, including locals Laurie Lee and Michael and Frances Horovitz (whose event the previous year had been 'bumped' by Yevtushenko). On the final night Charles Causley, Geoffrey Grigson and Seamus Heaney were the published attraction, and the 'authors of the ten leading entries in the poetry competition' were also promised. What an array!

Julian Barnes, sent to review the festival for the *New Statesman*, picked Doris Lessing's talk ('sombre and revealing') as a high point, but it was Christopher Ricks's lecture that eight years later he was to put into *Flaubert's Parrot*: 'His bald head was shiny; his black shoes were shiny; and his lecture was very shiny indeed. Its theme was Mistakes in Literature and Whether They Matter.'

All this took place in the Playhouse theatre down the road from the Town Hall. Small and slightly shabby, it was nevertheless a bona fide theatre with red plush and atmosphere. Most important of all, it is very hard for a performer not to be heard there.

In 1977 Ted Hughes appeared at the festival for the first time. Under the title of the Cheltenham Lecture, he talked about and read poetry by his favourite contemporary poets,

the new review

Editor: Ian Hamilton   11 Greek Street London W1V 6LE 01-437 4494, 439 4594

AN EVENING AT THE CHELTENHAM FESTIVAL
INTRODUCED BY IAN HAMILTON

PART ONE

Readings from The New Review by
JONATHAN RABAN
CRAIG RAINE
CHRISTOPHER REID
A. ALVAREZ

Interval

PART TWO

Introduced by Colin Falck, poetry critic
of The New Review
Readings by
PETER PORTER
JOHN FULLER
HUGO WILLIAMS
DOUGLAS DUNN

and

The World Premiere
of
IT'S DISGUSTING AT YOUR AGE
by
Martin Amis

Cast:
James .... John Flanagan
Freddie ...... Andrew McCulloch
Miranda ...... Sarah Beck
Felicity ..... Vivienne McKee

Lighting by   Tim Coates
Directed by   Richard Stroud

Programme for *The New Review* evening, 1977.

namely Zbigniew Herbert, Miroslav Holub, Yehuda Amichai and Vasco Popa. In this he fulfilled the director's stated intent of making it a festival of 'personal choices, personal views'. Dennis Potter was another first, as Doris Lessing had been the previous year. Ian Hamilton returned, bringing contributors to his magazine, now *The New Review*, with him. They are an impressive list – Jonathan Raban, Craig Raine, Christopher Reid and Al Alvarez read prose, then Peter Porter, John Fuller, Hugo Williams and Douglas Dunn poetry. Last and most memorably was a play by Martin Amis called *It's Disgusting at Your Age*, a comedy that hinged on the reversal of male/female stereotypes in the clubs, pubs and pads of the seventies. Serious reputations were reviewed and revived – the Powys brothers and Edward Thomas. And Andrew Motion and Craig Raine won that year's poetry competition with poems they had written on the same trip to Belfast.

The money raised by the 1977 poetry competition was enough for P.J. Kavanagh to instigate a new version of the Cheltenham Prize, this time to be an annual award of £250 given by a well-known reviewer to the writer of a book published that year which they considered had not received due attention. More resilient than its predecessor, it continued until 1994.

10 Naked in Cheltenham

One way and another the seventies had proved a struggle for the Festival of Literature. Audience figures had dropped. Cheltenham at large scarcely seemed to notice it taking place.

It had not known where to take place. The Everyman Theatre was expensive, the Playhouse too small for more popular events and neither had much room for book exhibitions or stalls. The Town Hall was more flexible, but there was the intractable problem of the acoustics. The search for a venue had pointed up the festival's nature as a hybrid: sometimes theatre, sometimes lecture, sometimes TV-like panel, sometimes poetry reading, sometimes celebrity interview . . . what did it need? Theatre? Lecture hall? Coffee bar? And books? What was a literature festival without books?

It had not known when to take place. The endeavour was to fit in with the schools and not to clash with the nearby Stroud Festival. Held for the first ten years in the first week of October, in 1969 it was moved to November. In 1975 it zoomed forward to the last week of September, before settling back into the first week of October. It was longer than the original festival – Sunday to Saturday, rather than Monday to Friday – but until P.J. Kavanagh's later festivals it still consisted of little more than seven evening events.

These questions came to a head with two pivotal festivals, 1978 and 1979, directed by a good-looking young chap with a moustache and kipper tie. He was A.C.H. Smith – novelist, scriptwriter, journalist and cricket reporter. Living in Bristol and dedicated to Cheltenham Gold Cup week, he was almost a local, having moved from London to take up a post with the *Western Daily Press*, where for some time he ran the Arts Page with Tom Stoppard.

Smith says that he is fascinated by the relationship between the written and spoken word. 'When I read a book, I hear it somewhere in my head and when I am writing I know I hear a narrative voice.' In his introduction to the 1978 festival he concluded: 'A festival of literature is a festival of the speaking voice, reciting, declaiming, arguing, narrating – a celebration of the English language.' He aimed to achieve 'a festival that is festive'.

His first festival largely followed the pattern of recent years: a couple of nights in the Everyman for the theatrical opener and a crowd-catcher on the second night (a theatre forum with Tom Stoppard, David Edgar and Geoffrey Reeves, then director of the Nottingham Playhouse), and the remaining five days at the Playhouse.

Two writers-in-residence, Eva Figes and Adrian Mitchell, took literature out to schools, colleges and prisons in Gloucestershire. Mitchell recorded and published a picaresque account of his progress in *Naked in Cheltenham*: schoolchildren 'sharp and open', whisky in the early hours at Anthony Smith's flat, no bath towel in his own, cruising the shelves in 'the shop of Alan Hancox, where old books go to be loved', drawings of writers by Alan's wife Shelagh, breakfast in Cavendish House, and . . .

A.C.H. Smith.

The trouble with writing a six day book:
You spend more and more time writing the book
Which is therefore liable to turn
Into a book about writing a book.

Anthony Smith's favourite memory is the evening that Michael Foot came to talk on Hazlitt. He had been delighted when Foot, whom he counts among his heroes, had written

Drawing of Anthony Smith by Shelagh Powys (Hancox) included by Adrian Mitchell in 'Naked in Cheltenham', 1978.

to say that he wanted to come to Cheltenham despite the fact that the Labour Party Conference in Blackpool only finished at noon the same day. The next letter was even better: Foot suggested he invite James Cameron, 'the greatest of the post-1945 journalists' as he once described him, so that if Foot was delayed Cameron could fill the gap. Anthony felt hesitant about asking if James Cameron – another of his heroes – would be prepared 'to sit on the subs bench', but the answer was positive. In the event there were no hitches. Michael Foot arrived, spoke 'like an angel' for exactly sixty minutes and without a single note. He then brought Cameron in and they 'went into this beautiful routine – two old friends who loved each other and also had very sharp minds. It was cream and the audience lapped it up.'

Afterwards the festival hosted dinner at the Queen's. They sat down at table, Michael Foot still talking as he had been ever since he arrived in Cheltenham. As they started the fish course, there was a loud thud. Michael Foot's head had just hit the table, narrowly missing his turbot. 'Don't worry', said Cameron, 'he'll be back with us in a few minutes. He's just very, very tired.' Ten minutes later, Foot woke up again. Talking.

This does indeed sound like 'a festival that is festive', but it made a financial loss. The Committee was worried and decided to reduce the festival to just four days, have more events on each day and move the date back again to November. The Town Hall was once more the main venue.

Anthony Smith invited Allen Ginsberg to be poet-in-residence for 1979. Ginsberg agreed, but wanted to bring another beat poet Peter Orlovsky and a musician with him. 'Come alone it'd be simpler for me, but this way it's more art + more pleasant tho much less profitable, + much more work to do', he wrote, with a characteristic blend of laid-back generosity and detail-picking practicality. He was to give a 'seminar on Meditation and Poetics' from 1–5 pm to 'allow 1½ hours talk and 2–3 hours accompanying sitting practice (i.e. a seminar about sitting includes sitting). . . . For the seminar we need an airy room or shaded tent with a rug and sitting cushions, or Zen-style Zafu, or some approximation of a small pillow.' They borrowed hassocks from a local church. Was it a sell-out? Smith admits he didn't stay himself, but then 'the Director doesn't have four hours to spare'. He describes their meeting: 'I was surprised to meet a middle-aged man dressed in a brown three-piece suit. But we hit it off, I loved him. He was immensely friendly. He would give one a bear hug each time one met him in the corridor. He did it all – workshops, schools, prisons – and seemed to enjoy it all.'

One evening Michael and Frances Horovitz and the jazz pianist Stan Tracey joined Ginsberg and retinue for an evening of poems and music. On another Conor Cruise O'Brien gave the Cheltenham Lecture on 'Religion, Politics and Literature' (attended by Ginsberg? Probably). Clive James and Russell Davies performed James's poem, 'Peregrine Prykke's Pilgrimage through the London Literary World', and Monty Python star Terry Jones spoke seriously about Chaucer despite the false nose he wore for the photograph in the brochure.

The winner of the 1979 festival, however, was an event that took its director completely by surprise. Pestered by a publisher friend, Smith had agreed to invite an author called Selma James. As he knew little of her except that she was a feminist and married to C.L.R. James, whose cricket writing he admired, he scheduled her talk 'Ms Jane Austen' for 'the graveyard slot' at noon on Sunday.

It was the last day, he was exhausted and he overslept. 'I woke up, realised it was ten to twelve, threw on my clothes and ran all the way to the Town Hall. When I got there the corridor was jammed with people. I pushed my way through and just got on stage in time to mutter a few words of welcome. She was sensational, quite quite brilliant. People wanted her to go on and on. I had had no idea she had such a huge following.'

The exhaustion was perhaps symptomatic of the feelings of responsibility and isolation he experienced as director. All the administration and practical arrangements were efficiently handled by the Town Hall staff, but looking after the authors and making sure they were having a good time was very much up to him. This is where he appreciated the help of Alan Hancox, then chairman of the Literature Committee, and his wife Shelagh. 'Alan was a tower to lean on. He and Shelagh were there most of the time and you knew they would automatically take up the slack if I had to rush away.'

Alan Hancox. (Leonard Hamilton)

Those who came to the 1979 festival found much to enjoy. Peter Orlovsky, Ginsberg's friend, went home to plant a walnut tree in memory of the good times. The problem was those that didn't come. Hardly covered at all by the local newspaper, a rare headline reads 'Ticket sales shock for festival'. No, not record-breaking, but surprisingly slow. 'Only six have been sold for one event', revealed the new festival organiser, Jeremy Tyndall.

The Committee met for the usual post-festival inquest. Serious questions were asked. Was it time to call it a day? Had the demand simply disappeared? Anthony Smith did not feel he had the ideas for another festival, so who could be the next director, if indeed one was needed? Names were being brought out and shuffled irresolutely, when Anthony stopped the talk, speaking with a degree of impatience. 'I don't know what you're talking about. It is perfectly obvious who you should appoint. He is sitting here in this room.' People looked at each other. Obvious?

'Your own chairman, Alan Hancox.'

Alan's first participatory involvement with the Literary Festival had been in 1955 when he put forward the poet W.S. Graham as a Guest Writer. He was invited to join the Committee in 1959. It was he who suggested Ian Hamilton as director for 1965–7, a step which he felt moved the festival on from a country-bound cosiness and brought poetry centre-stage.

In the afterglow of his great successes of the 1980s, people ask why Hancox was not appointed before. As early as 1965 Ian Hamilton had found him the mainstay of the festival, and was surprised when reminded that Alan only started directing in 1980. Certainly he would not have wanted to push himself forward, and just as certainly he would have been completely delighted to be asked. In fact P.J. Kavanagh had made the suggestion before, but the idea was quashed because Frank Littlewood, then chairman, felt they needed someone who cut more of a national figure.

Yet now, blinded as we are by hindsight, Alan seems the very embodiment of the Festival of Literature. Sonia Rolt, who knew Alan well both as a family friend and a fellow member of the Committee, says firmly, 'whatever one says about John Moore and all the others, it was Alan who made the festival what it is today'.

The qualifications are all there. The interest in books, awoken at the age of eighteen when Alan went to a WEA class and was given Tolstoy and Hardy to read – 'the deep end', as he put it. The love of countryside which he explored and shared as warden of the Cleeve Hill Youth Hostel, high on the Cotswold scarp above Cheltenham. Those were the days when every week he would walk the three miles into Winchcombe to buy books: 'I'd fill my rucksack and walk back over the hills, have a glass of beer, some bread and cheese.' Gradually he discovered special favourites – George Eliot, Hardy, D.H. Lawrence, John Cowper Powys, Edward Thomas, the Romantic poets, the Woolfs, Henry Williamson . . . the list became a long one.

He started to hold evenings of poetry and music at the Youth Hostel. Rosemary Hoggett, who knew Alan when she was a teenager, acknowledges her 'special debt' to him for 'he introduced me to T.S. Eliot and Dylan Thomas speaking their own poems . . . we would discuss these great poems with excitement, not understanding them, but being enthralled with their sounds and rhythms'.

He became a full-time bookseller in the late 1940s and published his first catalogue (of an eventual 150) in 1951. In 1966 he moved the shop to a basement on the Promenade, a stone's throw from the Town Hall, and bought a new house in the Bath Road area of Cheltenham. These became the venues for the readings and discussion groups of which he was so fond. Twenty or thirty people would regularly gather to hear a new poet and have a glass of wine. Melvyn Bragg speaks of Alan's 'book room' in his new home as 'my ideal for a room – panelled floor to ceiling with books of such ravishing content, title, binding, rarity . . . that you seem to sit in a glow of authors every bit as flickeringly mesmeric as the log fire.' Here Bragg spoke about *Jude the Obscure* on one of his first visits to Cheltenham. They developed a friendship over books, as Alan did with so many other writers and bibliophiles.

John Betjeman, so the story goes, inscribed all Alan's non-first editions of his books with 'I, John Betjeman, make this a first edition for Alan Hancox'. Michael Foot first came to the festival in 1970, a year with no ostensible director, when Alan received a vote of thanks from the Committee for his help with the programming. Whether the festival met Foot through Hancox or the other way round I do not know, but certainly he remained grateful: 'Alan taught me how to read Byron and to look for books about Byron. . . . The mystery is how he ever ran the book business at all because he was giving books away to everyone right left and centre.' For Michael's nephew Paul Foot, Alan would find treasures for his Shelley collection. For Ted Hughes, it would be Shakespeare. 'Alan was very good at finding the right book for the right person', says Shelagh Hancox. 'He was good at organising things. He had a huge capacity for work, and loved to start on new projects.' He liked to encourage young writers, particularly poets, and took an ongoing interest in their careers. His shop, his discussion groups and the festival were enough to make sure that he knew the literary people of the neighbour-hood.

So there we are. Alan knew the festival, he knew Cheltenham, he had passionate tastes in literature, was interested in new writing, he had organised literary events, he revered writers, had good contacts with several eminent authors, he was an excellent and persuasive letter writer (impossible, according to Miles Kington, to say 'no' to), and he was a businessman who knew the necessity for making the books balance. The festival had found its man.

Alan Hancox's bookshop seen from the Montpellier Street side.

11 COMING HOME

For Alan's first festival he programmed fifteen events in four days. It was a success: 2,046 tickets were sold, 500 more than the previous year. In 1990, Alan's last festival, there were sixty-five events in eight days. It was a triumph: 13,621 tickets sold, an all-time record. Events up fourfold, audience up almost sevenfold.

The story is not Alan's alone. He was stalwartly rivalled by Gordon Parsons, whose festivals wove between his own and built similar-sized audiences. Alan had known Gordon since 1958 when he arrived in Cheltenham to train to be a teacher at St Paul's College (later part of Cheltenham and Gloucester College of Higher Education). Gordon returned as a member of staff in 1968, the year he began his annual pilgrimages to the Edinburgh Festival. In 1977 he started to import his favourites and founded the Cheltenham Fringe Theatre for that purpose. For over ten years a 'fringe' production at the College's Shaftesbury Hall was the prelude to every Literature Festival.

The 1980 festival was the first to bring children to the centre of the festivities, which significantly livened up the atmosphere of the Town Hall. A 'Festival of Books for Children and Young Adults', opened by Monica Dickens, had been tried in the Old Bakery behind the library for a couple of years in 1971–2. A.C.H. Smith had revived the idea in 1978 when he invited a children's book expert and Bristol friend of his, Pat Triggs, to organise some 'happenings'. The following year these flowered into a full-blown Children's Book Fair with a Victorian town trail, a drama workshop, competitions, exhibitions and bookstall, and appearances by Dorothy Edwards and Shirley Hughes, jointly responsible for the *My Naughty Little Sister* books, and long-term festival supporter, Ursula Moray Williams (author of *The Little Wooden Horse*). The success was such as to cause it to be moved into the Town Hall where in 1980 it attracted over 3,000 children – who watched the Revd Awdry, creator of Thomas the Tank Engine and friends, demonstrate his electric train set; who dressed up in Regency costume for a 'rout' at the Pump Room; who were tickled by the zany poems of Michael Rosen, and listened to Winifred Foley talk about her Forest of Dean childhood. Organised by the local children's librarian, Michael Darling, schools were encouraged to send parties to weekday events. Children came with their parents at weekends.

Children at the 'Regency Rout' in front of the Pump Rooms, 1980. (Courtesy of the *Gloucestershire Echo*)

During the 1980s Michael Darling's 'Family Fun Weekends' were to become an established feature of the festival, joined in 1987 by the W.H. Smith Schools' Festival, which involved 1,600 pupils in workshops and performances across Gloucestershire. Children were now often in the majority, overwhelming the literary faithful as they poured down the corridors, balloons bobbing, clutching the results of a workshop session or laden with freebies handed out by willing publicists.

Queenie Leavis opened Alan's first festival with the Cheltenham Lecture on 'The Englishness of the English Novel', reputedly a better performance than her husband's inaugural lecture twelve years before. By then seventy-three, white-haired and frail, she kept the audience in thrall for an hour. She was touchingly thrilled by the enthusiasm with which they applauded her and said 'for two pins she'd have given an encore'. Colin Wilson, whom Alan knew to be a speaker of 'magnificent enthusiasm', was given an open-ended slot for his talk on 'Literature and Mysticism' so that he could supply encores galore.

But 1980 brought an unexpected shock. Alan was diagnosed with renal failure. He was told that he might not live more than three years. Shelagh Hancox says his response was to ignore his medical condition as far as he could (not easy considering he was on dialysis) and turn his mind to other things. She says that the festival gave him purpose. With the knowledge that each festival was potentially his last, he directed the next two years with enthusiasm and growing confidence, a man getting truly into his stride.

Revd Wilbert Awdry, creator of *Thomas the Tank Engine,* at the 1980 festival. (Courtesy of the *Gloucestershire Echo*)

The festival that took off was the 31st in 1981. Jeremy Tyndall, who had become organiser for both the Music and Literature Festivals, in 1979 (although he had no idea there was a Literature Festival until midway through his job interview), remembers that audience figures leapt when there was a much-publicised brouhaha about Enoch Powell's appearing at Cheltenham to speak on George Borrow.

The story begins on the Saturday. Alan had handed that day over to Michael Horovitz for a Poetry Olympics, like one which Horovitz had recently organised in Westminster Abbey. It ran an extraordinary gamut of poetry – from Robert Gittings on John Keats at 11 am, through U.A. Fanthorpe and Laurie Lee, washed down with free Guinness (as always generous to poetry), on to a polyphony of poets across continents (including China), to arrive in the evening at an 'Internationale of the Spirit' which included Heathcote Williams on elephants, a rare appearance by Elizabeth Smart, author of *By Grand Central Station I Sat Down and Wept*, and R.D. Laing, described in the brochure as 'anti-psychiatrist extraordinaire'.

The trouble focused on the final event, a late-nighter with Jamaican-born poet Linton Kwesi Johnson and John Cooper Clarke. The local papers shrieked 'I won't share a stage with Powell says black poet', 'Festival row over Enoch Powell'. The *Guardian* picked it up. Michael Horovitz, anti-Establishment poet and kazoo-playing impresario of countercultural events, found himself in a dilemma. It was much the same as the one described by the *Sunday Telegraph* magazine when he was one of the judges for the 1977 Cheltenham Poetry Competition: 'Horovitz is anti-Establishment; poems that win Establishment prizes are Establishment poems: how could he acclaim a winning poem without admitting it to the Establishment he loathes.' He opined that Powell should only ever be allowed to speak publicly on George Borrow, and the following day, no longer on duty, joined the picket outside the Town Hall (rather than the now large queue to get in).

And how did all this start? On that Saturday Linton Kwesi Johnson was supposed to be at the Frankfurt Book Fair. He rang to apologise and suggested he might be able to appear on the Sunday if there was space. In the course of the telephone call Johnson found out about Enoch Powell and quickly refused to take part at all.

The 1982 festival was opened by Marghanita Laski, now chairman of the Arts Council Literature Panel, who introduced an enormous and well-remembered exhibition of *Literary Portraits*, the private collection of Roy Davids of Sotheby's. It was held in the Thirlestaine Long Gallery at Cheltenham College. The opening lasted all Sunday afternoon with a talk on Yeats followed by a performance based on Kilvert's *Diary*. Of twenty-six events that year, eleven were talks or performances dedicated to literary figures of the past, and fifteen featured living writers. At the Town Hall there were exhibitions of work by local artists and a display of antiquarian books. At weekends late-night music, poetry and talk were provided free. That year several of Alan's favourite speakers were in town – Melvyn Bragg, Paul Foot, Seamus Heaney and Ted Hughes, the latter two stealing the show with a sell-out reading in the Main Hall on the Saturday night. 'Not everyone could hear it all,' said Alan, 'but it really didn't seem to matter.'

It was hailed as 'the best ever', an achievement made poignant by the fact that Alan had been badly ill in hospital in September. At his suggestion Gordon Parsons was appointed director for 1983 and – as it turned out – for 1984 as well.

'The Edinburgh Festival was my inspiration. It was that excitement and atmosphere that I wanted to recreate in Cheltenham. I was full of ideas, you know how you are, the first time. Alan had asked me to do a series of events centred around drama for 1982, and I was on the Festival Committee, so I was pretty familiar with it all. I loved the excitement of those first letters back, the first yeses.'

Demonstrators outside Cheltenham Town Hall waiting for Enoch Powell, 1981. (Courtesy of the *Gloucestershire Echo*)

Peggy Ashcroft's was one of them. For a lifelong enthusiast of the theatre such as Gordon, it was a moving moment when she insisted that she read his carefully penned introduction out loud at the opening party: 'A Festival of Literature should celebrate literature and reaffirm its relevance and importance to the world outside the book. Surely in our time of crisis . . .'. Impeccably cadenced, the words dropped into the crowded room.

Another 'yes' was A.J.P. Taylor. His original letter warned 'This is a provisional offer. We must agree on a subject, probably history as literature which would be fun. We must agree on a fee which should not be difficult. There is also the possibility that I may be unfit. I am not the man I was five or ten years ago but I should be all right.' Subject was agreed, fee agreed, but in September came sad news: 'I have developed a severe form of Parkinson's disease which makes it quite impossible for me to appear in public.'

A. L. Rowse stepped in, as he had almost 30 years before when Margaret Irwin fell ill. Parsons had approved Taylor's suggestion of 'History as Literature', so it was this that Rowse spoke on. Did he or anyone in the audience remember that his stand-in lecture of 1954 had exacly the same title? On that occasion he dealt mostly with Carlyle; this was an exposition on Shakespeare's sexual interests, interspersed with jibes against 'third-class historians'.

Innovations of 1983 were the '£1 Ploughman's and Poetry' (free cheese roll and cider provided) sessions among paintings and sculpture in the Art Gallery & Museum, Andrew Motion and Liz Lochhead among the participants, and the Shakespeare Lecture, invented by Gordon and programmed by him for the next six years with the idea of alternately inviting actors and academics. A personal triumph was persuading Michael Hordern, who had recently published a book on fishing, to talk about Izaac Walton and *The Compleat Angler*. P.J. Kavanagh gave a poetry reading with fellow Cotswoldian Charles Tomlinson. In his letter accepting the invitation, Patrick gave Gordon a kindly warning: 'I hope you don't expect *any* Festival to be as successful as last year's which included everything as well as the kitchen stove. Impossible to follow, I reckon. Personally I wouldn't try. Would tell everybody mine is going to be *less* successful!' Less can be more, but Gordon's festival, hailed by the *Echo* as 'literature for the masses', had the audacity to exceed the previous year's box office by 900 tickets.

As the largest source of revenue, ticket sales were vital. Alan had realised this and programmed accordingly. He had also cut back on expenses by encouraging local supporters to host the writers rather than putting them in hotels, and by giving the select among them books rather than fees, his personal form of subsidy to the festival.

At this date South West Arts were not happy with what they saw as the commercialisation of Cheltenham, nor – as ever – with the level of financial support from the County or the Borough, despite the fact that, run within the Council, Cheltenham Arts Festivals enjoys a considerable 'hidden subsidy'. As a member of the South West Arts panel, P.J. Kavanagh did his best to promote the interests of the festival, but it seems to have been regarded as a rather large cuckoo among smaller clients. Alan had sought sponsorship – Sotheby's had begun supporting the Cheltenham Lecture, the newly local European Schoolbooks had taken on Pushkin in 1981, Guinness and Whitbread had given beer and parties, publishers were contributing to their authors' expenses, the National Poetry Secretariat (after 1982 the Poetry Society) gave grants for poetry. But it was in 1983 that a chance encounter changed the festival's approach to funding.

Gordon Parsons.

Gordon had programmed a debate on 'The Influence of Marxism on Literature'. Colin McCabe, a leading proponent of structuralism in English Literature at the time, was among the panellists. A satisfactorily lively discussion under the chairmanship of John Spurling, playwright and reviewer for the *New Statesman*, had taken place and the speakers were in the bar, trying to listen to or shred conversation through 'Rastafari Wordsong and Music' supplied by poet Shakka Dedi and friends. Gordon felt a tap on his shoulder. He turned round.

'Are you the director?' He nodded, easier than making himself heard.

'Will you be the director next year?'

'I hope to be.' The man was beaming at him, patent goodwill emanating through striped shirt and well-cut suit.

'Well, I'd like to help you with raising sponsorship. I'm Charles Fisher, a friend of Colin McCabe's. I haven't been before and I think it's terrific what you're doing. Here's my card.'

Several weeks later, appointed for 1984, Gordon rang Charles Fisher and went to see him for lunch at the head offices of Sharpe & Fisher, a name once familiar ('grate people') from the sides of Cheltenham's double-decker buses, now the leading builders' merchants in the south-west.

'It was extraordinary', said Gordon. 'He was offering to take on the sponsorship side. I had been trudging round to local businesses and coming out with a cheque for £25 if I was lucky. I heard Charles get on the phone and say "I have a variety of things here to offer you from £500 to £1,000". And he would get it, just like that.'

From now on sponsorship became an increasingly important part of the Literature Festival's income. Charles Fisher's dynamism shook up the whole of Cheltenham Arts Festivals. A development committee was formed for both Music (which had already gone some way down the sponsorship path) and Literature Festivals and the rules for membership of the Board and Committees were amended to allow more flexibility for new members to come in.

12 THE 'BEST EVER'

n 1984 Paul Foot spoke on George Orwell. A panel examined the state of the nation's literary health. Afterwards Marghanita Laski took David Edgar's mackintosh home by mistake. Frances Horovitz's life was celebrated for she had died the year before – the woman of whom everybody immediately said, 'Oh, Frances was lovely!' and 'She had such a beautiful voice. Her readings were exquisite.' Dr Johnson's life was celebrated for he had died two hundred years before – with a talk by John Wain followed by a specially written dramatisation starring Timothy West. Oppressed writers were remembered in a benefit for *Index on Censorship*, introduced by Stephen Spender with readings by Billie Whitelaw. Max Wall performed Beckett's *Malone Dies*, the talk of that year's Edinburgh Festival. The audience eddied round the twin themes Gordon had taken up: censorship and criticism.

The 1985 festival burst upon Cheltenham packed with all the inventive energy of Alan's two years in the wings. It also had a theme: 'The Spirit of Place in Literature'. On the front cover of the brochure was a drawing of Alan at his typewriter, open hills and wooded valleys wafting out of the keys. Above his head ran the names of the speakers he had secured – more than ever before – and above them a dancing man with panpipes, the woodcut by Helmut Weissenborn that Alan had adopted to symbolise the festival.

The 'genius loci' idea had apparently come to Alan when he was reading Edward Thomas on Cleeve Hill, the highest point in the Cotswolds, as he looked down across the panoramic view to the west – Cheltenham beneath him, the Severn Valley stretched out beyond, blocking the horizon the Malverns and May Hill (where Thomas walked with Robert Frost), in the far distance Wenlock Edge, the Black Mountains and Hay Bluff. He thought of all the writers who had occupied that landscape: Kilvert, Housman, W.H. Davies, Ivor Gurney, H.E. Massingham, James Elroy Flecker . . . now Tomlinson, Kavanagh, U.A. Fanthorpe, Jenny Joseph, Peter Levi . . . and he thought more generally of writers in their special places – Dylan Thomas at Laugharne, Yeats at Ballylee, Colin Wilson in Cornwall, Laurie Lee nearby in the Slad Valley. So he invited Melvyn Bragg to create a day on Wordsworth, Seamus Heaney to speak on Yeats and his Tower, and poet Roger Garfitt to talk on Heaney and Ireland. He asked Michael Foot (to whom he gave the soubriquet 'patron saint of our festival') to do 'Byron in Venice', Paul Foot 'Shelley', Peter

Toasting the 1984 festival: director Gordon Parsons and administrator Jeremy Tyndall with G. Wilson Knight and Stephen Spender. (Courtesy of the *Gloucestershire Echo*)

Levi (then Oxford Professor of Poetry) 'Eliot's England'. E.P. Thompson talked about Blake, and Ronald Blythe covered 'Divine Landscapes', especially John Clare's.

The 'spirit of place' was a theme that encouraged the use of new venues. Since 1980 Alan and Gordon had been beginning the festival outside the Town Hall: in country churches, tithe barns and church halls, as well as places such as Shaftesbury Hall and schools in Cheltenham itself. As part of 'Around and About Gloucestershire' Prunella Scales and Benjamin Whitrow scored a hit with John Betjeman's *Church Poems* in Bishop's Cleeve church, Barbara Leigh-Hunt and Richard Pasco brought Hardy to Winchcombe church, James Elroy Flecker was celebrated in Leckhampton church where he is buried, and local poet F.W. Harvey was recalled in the Forest of Dean.

Melvyn Bragg devoted three weeks' worth of his column in *Punch* to Alan and the 1985 festival. He described Paul Foot's 'irresistible hectoring style which had the Cheltenham audience rocking on the Town Hall seats' as Foot beat back Shelley's detractors. Billed as Wordsworth's man, Melvyn felt obliged to beard Paul afterwards over a cup of coffee. 'And what might be called the subtext of the next two days began: partly through the passion brought to it by Foot, partly due to the presence there of those who could extend and develop that argument, drop it, lead it into other territories – to Yeats with Seamus Heaney, for instance, to Auden in the practically all-night session back *chez* Hancox . . . what happened was that the ground was cleared for a widely admitted exchange between writers, readers, critics, bookmen – on the public and the private, the intimate, the detailed, the external, the obvious.' He called Alan and Shelagh's house – where many of them stayed, and where the book room was in constant use for rehearsal room, solitary refuge, afternoon salon, party venue or late-night drinking den – 'the social fulcrum of

Drawing of Alan Hancox in 1985. (Chris Hoggett)

literary Cheltenham'. Even Edinburgh, he said drawing to his conclusion, 'has not, in my experience, provided such a fertile play between the watchers and the performers'.

In one year, the festival had again doubled in size. Over 11,000 seats sold. Thirty-six years on, the numbers had at last exceeded the record of 7,000 set by the first, John Moore's festival in 1949.

'Laurels for Laurie', a tribute to Laurie Lee, brought the 1986 festival to an end on a high note. Alan had woken in the small hours one night in June and thought of letters he had received from Laurie: 'One of them contained the brief but sad (I thought) comment that you were getting old and putting yourself to rest.' Alan wanted to celebrate 'the fact that you are still with us . . . a sort of personification of changelessness in this mostly ghastly changing world . . . for once you do not have to DO anything, just come & sit in a dark corner (in disguise if you like). . . . It will all be "done" properly & the three bars will be open before, during and after, with booze and goodwill flowing freely.' Alan enlisted the help of Cathy, Laurie's wife, and his publisher and collected in a mass of poems and writings from his friends. As it turned out it was not goodbye, for Lee eventually said that in 1994 at the conclusion of a touching interview with Edward Blishen, suddenly standing the better to address the vastness of his audience directly.

Gordon Parsons and Alan Hancox programmed the 1986 festival together. Gordon remembers that they would meet for a working lunch at Alan's once a week. He did not always find it an easy partnership. It was a situation in which he was likely to experience the 'quarrel' in Alan that Seamus Heaney was later to describe so well, between 'a part that was brusque and impatiently intelligent and anti-bullshit and very on the move and another part that was reticent and intuitive and full of intimacy'. Despite the fact that the theme was 'Literature and Theatre', Gordon's speciality, Alan was inclined to feel that he was the one who had done all the work. But like so many others Gordon was to say 'I had known Alan for years and I loved him'.

Because the Town Hall was being redecorated, the festival took place appropriately in the Everyman Theatre, itself recently reopened after several years of refurbishment.

Behind the scenes – stage, offices, a new studio theatre-cum-rehearsal room, and workshops – had been entirely rebuilt and enlarged as part of the new development that replaced the Plough Hotel with Cheltenham's first shopping mall. The façade had had its sixties modernity stripped away and been restored to a eighties version of the restrained original. Jeremy Tyndall remembers that fitting sixty-six events in quick succession into the theatre was a challenge. The studio, the bar, even the stage area separated off by the 'iron', were brought into service for smaller events. The foyers and stairways were packed with people, but still the atmosphere was not the same without the Children's Book Fair, moved for lack of space to the Axiom Gallery up the road.

It was the year of the worst event ever. Auberon Waugh, Peter Cook, Paul Theroux and other contributors to the *Literary Review* were billed to discuss, in a frivolous sort of way, the future of literary rags. The panel was entirely unprepared. Peter Cook sat with his back to the audience. The editor Auberon Waugh, bolstered by many lovely young women in red sashes, treated it as a sales pitch. Humphrey Carpenter, next on the billing, anticipated a bleak reception for his band Vile Bodies as more and more empty seats clacked shut.

The summer of 1987 the Friends of the Literature Festival were inaugurated at a reading by Seamus Heaney, their first patron. Their aims were very similar to the Literary Festival Society of thirty years earlier – to raise money, to support the festival with practical help such as accommodation, stewarding and driving, and to organise events and social occasions through the year. In the early years, it was another outlet for Alan's never-ending flow of ideas. A beautiful series of small posters featuring poems by Heaney, Lee, Jenny Joseph, and Lawrence Sail on the theme of the elements, illustrated by woodcuts and printed by John Randle of the Whittington Press, proved popular with collectors. Other merchandise was planned, designed and made by Shelagh Hancox and artist friends such as Jane Bywater, Charmaine and Terry Murphy and Chris Hoggett. The Friends' stall became a regular feature of the festival.

Gordon Parsons, director of 1987, depressed by the paucity of books the previous year, instigated 'The World of Books' in the Main Hall. He invited three booksellers to set out their wares. There were three exhibitions – a Festival of Illustration, children's books from the Opie Collection and Twentieth-Century Classics selected by Margaret Drabble, and café tables were set out. Large events were to be put on in the Everyman.

'Theatrical events, as usual, were the most popular', read the director's report afterwards, although his personal highlight was George Steiner, who gave the Cheltenham Lecture on 'Constraints', an examination of aesthetic and social censorship, written specially for the festival during three days of walking in Switzerland. Monica Dickens, who revealed her work with the Samaritans, was the audience's favourite. Jack Klaff, whom Gordon had first seen in Edinburgh, and who had premiered his one-man *Kafka* at the festival, was 'resident writer and artist' for the week. There were twenty-four theatrical events, most of them one-man shows.

Ted Hughes and Alan
Hancox at the 1990
festival.
(Michael Charity)

An actor not featured in 1987 was Peter Florence, who first came to the festival in 1983 to perform his *Pity of War* adapted from the poems of Wilfred Owen. But it was the year that Peter Florence's father came to Cheltenham to talk to Gordon and Alan about the Florences' idea of holding a literature festival in Hay-on-Wye, the small border town set in lush green hills, already famous for its books. Alan was always delighted to set someone off on a new enterprise – he'd encouraged several acquaintances to take up bookselling – and he would always treasure the card acknowledging his help that Peter Florence sent him on the occasion of the first Hay-on-Wye Festival in 1988. This wasn't to say that Alan did not feel fiercely competitive when his protegé proved itself Cheltenham's most serious challenger.

Since 1949 Cheltenham had remained the only regular 'purely literary festival' until Ilkley started twenty-four years later. Cambridge Poetry Festival began soon after and Lancaster followed in 1978, but it was only in the 1980s that literary festivals began to pop up all over the place: Birmingham Readers and Writers, Cardiff, Huddersfield, Kings Lynn, Kent, Newcastle, Berkshire, Shrewsbury. Established multi-art festivals such as Brighton started to feature literary events or even spawned separate progeny: the biennial Edinburgh Book Fair in 1983, the Aldeburgh Poetry Festival in 1988.

Hay quickly established that it too could attract large audiences to hear writers. A tented town was provided, less formal than Cheltenham's salubrious halls and with better sound, unless the wind or rain battered too loudly on the canvas. The backdrop to the picturesque streets of Hay was the lovely intimacy of the Welsh hills. The *Sunday Times* sponsored and promoted it vigorously.

Cheltenham's Literature Festival realised that it was being presented with a choice: rest on the laurels of the 1980s, or enter the race for the 1990s. Or that was how some people saw it. Charles Fisher ran into an old friend, the writer Nicholas Shakespeare, then working for the *Daily Telegraph*, at a country house party. Despite the fact that Shakespeare immediately claimed to 'loathe literary festivals', Charles contacted him afterwards. The idea landed up on Marilyn Warnick's desk, in charge at the time of the *Telegraph*'s book publications. Seeing an opportunity to develop the paper's reputation for its book reviews and coverage, and with Cheltenham – as she puts it – 'in the heartland of *Telegraph* readership', she went to the editor Max Hastings, who encouraged her to visit the 1990 festival.

By now Alan had the 1988 Festival under his belt and Gordon had taken on 1989, which he had dedicated to 'Tradition and Revolution'. It turned out to be his favourite. The 1990 festival was Alan Hancox's last, the swan song of a decade of swan songs. It was the 'best ever', both in his opinion and many other people's. He put it down to good writers who were also good speakers, well-read audiences asking good questions. 'Suddenly it caught fire on the third day, and audiences doubled in the week that followed', he said. Angela Carter, Edna O'Brien, William Golding, Christopher Fry, Paul Bailey, Penelope Fitzgerald, Fay Weldon, E.P. Thompson, Ronald Blythe, Germaine Greer, Tariq Ali, A.S. Byatt, Marina Warner, Colin Wilson, Malcolm Bradbury, Terry Pratchett, John Mortimer, Richard Ingrams, Joseph Brodsky and James Fenton were some of those who responded to Alan's invitation to his 'retrospective'. And of course his band of faithfuls were there: Melvyn Bragg, Seamus Heaney, Michael Foot, Paul Foot and Ted Hughes. A file full of letters is evidence of the tremendous gratitude, affection and support given to Alan by those that came.

13 EXPANSION!

With the support of Max Hastings, Charles Fisher and Marilyn Warnick, the staff of Cheltenham Arts Festivals successfully negotiated a deal to bring the *Daily Telegraph* on board as the festival's sponsor for 1991. The good news was delivered to the Management Committee. They wanted none of it.

If the festival had a leaning in the 1980s, it was definitely towards the Left. Surrounded by *Telegraph* readers, inhabitants of a town burdened by a reputation for blue rinses and elderly colonels, the *Guardian*-reading intelligentsia of Cheltenham, who had been part of fostering not only a literature festival, but also an international music festival dedicated from its very roots to supporting contemporary composers, did not want to reinforce the popular image of their town as a sort of Tory joke. Some saw the advantage or even necessity for the money and media support that the *Telegraph* could offer, but many were nervous that their festival would be changed beyond recognition. To the bemused disbelief of all who had worked to win the sponsorship, it took some time to persuade a reluctant Committee to accept a three year deal and a substantial sum of money.

For many years the Committee had been under the thumb of Alan Hancox, a swing away from the 1970s when directors submitted their ideas diffidently for approval and obediently chased suggestions. One difference between Alan and other directors was that he knew more about the Literature Festival than any other human being, whether festival employee or long-term devotee. Even so, many members of the Committee knew it almost as well as he: Lucile Bell (formerly Moore), Heather Newman, Sonia Rolt, Paul Humphreys, P.J. Kavanagh – most had been involved for twenty years or more and had seen it through its slumps as well as its successes. The same was true of the second generation Borough Council employees who served the festivals: Keith Nutland, treasurer for many years, was a wizard for fixing the figures so they told the right story; Brian Wynn, Town Clerk and thus secretary to the festivals 1973–91, was another quiet champion, veteran of many a difficult meeting, who says he arrived when 'to an outsider the festival appeared to be dying on its knees'.

In 1991 the Literature Festival was still the little sister to the Music Festival, which bore more of the staffing costs within its much larger budgets which had to be substantial

John Mortimer,
Alan Hancox and
Michael Foot with
festival organiser
Kim Sargeant
(behind), 1990.
(Michael Charity)

enough to pay professional musicians. John Manduell, artistic director of the Music Festival since 1969, and one of the most influential figures on the Board, paid his first visit to the Literature Festival in 1984, an indication of how deeply it had been lost in the shadow of the Music Festival earlier.

The staffing of the festivals had gradually expanded during the 1980s. Jeremy Tyndall said he 'almost died' under the pressure of the 1983 festivals, when the Music Festival put on Lennox Berkeley's opera *Ruth* and the Literature Festival was getting more elaborate with every year. He had to bring in temporary help, and in 1986 Kim Sergeant was appointed organiser for both festivals. A sponsorship & development coordinator was appointed and began the fundraising enterprise that today attracts national awards and draws on the support and interest of well over 50 local businesses each year. I was employed part-time in 1991 to help with the Literature Festival, the first-ever member of staff to work for it alone. The Festivals had always called on the services of the Town Hall publicity officer, but it was found increasingly necessary to bring in freelancers to work with the national press. The bookshop has eventually settled down, run from a more or less adequate home in a marquee at the back of the Town Hall by Waterstones and Hammicks in tandem.

How can I describe what happened in the next nine years?

Supported by the *Daily Telegraph* until 1996, then by the *Independent*, the Cheltenham Festival of Literature in the nineties has broken into a different league. The 1992 festival added over 10,000 to the size of the 13,000-strong adult audience that Alan had attracted

IVOR GURNEY CENTENARY

1890 · 1937

P.J. Kavanagh and
Lawrence Sail, 1990.
(Michael Charity)

to his 'best-ever' two years before. If events for children and young people were included, the 1992 total came to over 30,000. Each successive year has brought an increase – particularly the last two – and the latest figures have topped 41,000.

Obviously this did not happen overnight. Lawrence Sail – poet and critic – had become involved in the festival during the 1980s. Editor of *South West Review* and judge for the Poetry Competition in 1982, he later became chairman of the Arvon Foundation, that pioneering provider of writing workshops. In 1990 the Management Committee, looking for a change of direction and inspired by his proposal for a festival with a European theme, appointed him director for 1991. Invitations went out to key writers in twenty European countries. Lawrence Sail trudged round the embassies seeking the money and diplomatic contacts that would get the speakers over to the UK. The British Council and the Visiting Arts Unit stepped in very generously to help. The result was that twenty-eight writers, many of them poets and all highly thought of in their own countries – Finland, Germany, Bulgaria, Serbia, Austria, Poland, Hungary, Romania, Sweden and Denmark – were booked for Cheltenham. The problem was that even the most famous of them, Ryszard Kapuscinski, Nina Cassian, Gert Hofmann, Gunter Kunert (back after 26 years), were pitifully ill-known to the generality of the UK reading public. The Europeans were matched by a sparkling list of English-speaking poets, short story writers and academics.

Lawrence Sail remembers that he wanted to create a festival that was not full of 'the usual suspects' and felt that much would depend on good publicity, so the *Daily Telegraph*'s support was crucial. He was aware that it was a special moment in history. With the Wall down, Europe was holding its breath in anticipation of what would happen next. There were great hopes that translators and publishers would get to work to disseminate literature across language barriers like never before. In 1991 it was an unexpected delight to listen to poetry in a completely foreign tongue, to witness the pleasure of writers free to mix with each other, to hear them with the translators who had unlocked their words for the West. Lawrence introduced and summarised every event with a poet's attentive dexterity and generally made sure that everyone – from behind-the-scenes helper to star performer – was happy.

It was now, with the encouragement of the *Daily Telegraph* which was launching the *Young Telegraph* as a Saturday supplement, that the Children's Festival got a big boost. Under the directorship of local educationalist John Haynes it was renamed 'Book It!' and given brightly coloured billing in the main brochure. Big names such as Harry Secombe and Rolf Harris had the Town Hall completely overrun with children. Paddington Bear and Peter Rabbit would tangle with poets on their way to a lunchtime reading. The caterers made slime-like jelly and Turtle pizzas.

Nevertheless all this did not make it the mainstream jamboree of 1990 that had captivated the *Daily Telegraph* whose level of support Lawrence felt was disappointing. Germaine Greer, Stephen Fry, Richard Eyre and John Julius Norwich were added to the adult programme, but with the Main Hall occupied by exhibitions and books, European flags hung from every balcony, capacity for the most popular event was only 350.

'Book It!' Children's Festival: Rolf Harris in 1993. (Jan McMillan)

This was the context for the choice of 1992 director, and the *Daily Telegraph* thought that publisher Richard Cohen might be the man the festival needed. Olympic fencer, theatre enthusiast, father of three then smallish bookreaders, he was much spoken of at the time as Jeffrey Archer's chosen editor, so the deduction was that he was not allergic to blockbusters. More important were the number and variety of other authors – from Mike Brearley to Fay Weldon – he had edited and commissioned, for contacts such as these could be the backbone of his festival. He arrived for interview with the Management Committee and presented his thoughts for a rich plum-pudding of a festival.

For some events he turned to friends whom he knew to be particularly eloquent on their subject: biographers Richard Holmes, Victoria Glendinning and Hilary Spurling fell into this group. For others he picked things up from the grapevine: Elisabeth Maxwell, not long widowed, spoke about letter-writing (which enraged Max Hastings and the Maxwell pensioners), Dirk Bogarde read from his latest book, Fay Weldon's broken marriage fuelled a feeling attack on therapists. Cohen located ideas that interested speakers and matched them to his themes – letter-writing, psychology and literature, questions about the current state of British writing, politics, crime, history. His interest in theatre, dating back to his schooldays, inspired his invention of the Youth Drama Festival, whereby four dramatists were commissioned to write plays for local schools and work with them towards their performance at the festival. Supported from the outset by UCAS, which is based in Cheltenham, the Drama Festival is now in its eighth year, recharged every year by a crop of new ideas and the talents of young people from all over Gloucestershire.

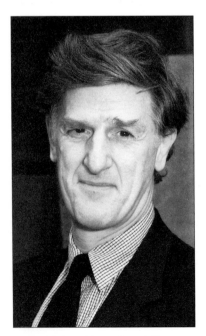

Richard Cohen. (Susan Greenhill)

In many ways it was a festival that picked up the Hancox tradition, and it seemed right that it began with Alan, who had died earlier in 1992. Seamus Heaney, Michael Foot, Ted Hughes and Melvyn Bragg remembered him clearly and movingly. Alan would have been thrilled by the size of the audience, and by the buzz that was already stirring the air. The press had picked up on the Maxwell story, Kevin had been seen slipping quietly down the corridor to slip into his mother's lecture shortly after it began. The BBC's John Simpson, Martha Gellhorn (who claimed she had never done such a thing before and insisted on taking whisky and cigarettes on stage) and the *Telegraph*'s Max Hastings had just electrified the audience with a discussion of war reporting. Later Anthony Burgess delivered the first European Lecture, a talk on translation, demonstrating a virtuoso knowledge of most of the languages in the world. With remarkable candour he announced: 'I am myself shortly to be translated', revealing that he had just been diagnosed as terminally ill with cancer.

In his *Spectator* column P.J. Kavanagh, veteran of so many Cheltenham Festivals of Literature, reviewed this one with a grand enthusiasm. At a reading given by poets Kit Wright (exceptionally tall, skilled performer) and Elizabeth Jennings (small, very shy, festival Guest Writer in 1956), he discerned a 'tangible wave of warmth and affection the huge audience sent up to her on the platform. . . . She began nervously, and ended radiant. She was among friends.' He went on, 'From then on the engine rolled, the wide Town Hall corridors packed like rush-hour tube-trains between events; and this odd sense of a mutually generated excitement.'

Heather Spears' drawing of Kurt Vonnegut at the 1993 festival.

Canadian artist and poet, Heather Spears, drew instantly recognisable sketches of the performers and pinned them down one corridor: punctuated memories of the week as it progressed. Jung Chang held up her grandmother's tiny shoes for us all to see. A queue of women, eager to tell Dirk Bogarde (matinée idol for thirty years) how much they loved him, snaked patiently round inside the entire building. A rivalry broke out between Jeffrey Archer and his wife Mary, ex-Cheltenham Ladies' College girl, over who would get the larger audience for their talks on the last day (she did). Stephen Pile, who wrote a diary every day for the *Daily Telegraph*, became a fellow survivor in the marathon we were all running that week, exhausted but still smiling. Richard Cohen, on stage over and over again to welcome and thank, spoke with courtly good manners enhanced by flights of humour. Behind the scenes one might find him less formal, grabbing ten seconds for half a sandwich, a Lion bar and a carton of orange juice. The end was a party of congratulations, everyone happy – sponsors, Committee, organisers, audience.

The success of his first festival was the springboard that encouraged Richard Cohen to go for an ambitious second – a celebration of North American writing that brought forty US and Canadian authors to Cheltenham. Most memorable was Kurt Vonnegut, who almost pulled out when there was confusion over his airline tickets in New York, and then sent possibly the shortest fax in history with the news he would come after all: 'OK. K.V.';

who finished his lecture with a eulogy on the leisurely pleasures of posting a manuscript from his local post office: 'I am here to tell you that we are here on earth to fart around'; who was scheduled to speak on Hemingway and Fitzgerald, but did not come back from London (Claridges again), necessitating a valiant Jilly Cooper to console and divert his audience. Joseph Heller made up for it all by being a kindly, funny and helpful presence all week.

Gore Vidal said that he hated literature festivals but appeared to like this one better once a lot of people had told him how wonderful he was. A big party stayed at Sudeley Castle with Lady Ashcombe, who gave a sumptous dinner in their honour. Margaret Atwood delivered the Cheltenham Lecture. Frances Partridge, aged ninety-three and Bloomsbury's last survivor, gave an immaculate talk about diary writing, one of the themes of that year. With *Birdsong* on course for the bestseller lists, Sebastian Faulks joined a discussion on war journals with Roy Hattersley and John Keegan and gave a talk on Wilfred Owen, a late addition not advertised in the brochure. Allen Ginsberg returned to Cheltenham. He was forty minutes late for his first appearance, due to being stuck on the train from London, but seemed entirely unworried – unlike me. The *New Yorker* magazine hosted a day. They flew in a panoply of writers and cartoonists, provided Martin Amis when Muriel Spark could not come, gave a chic reception, and put up their brightest team to meet Peregrine Worsthorne, Charles Moore and Mary Kenny from the *Sunday Telegraph* for a no-holds-barred debate about the sixties, chaired with impious partiality by John Mortimer.

Allen Ginsberg arrives at last heralded by Nicola Bennett, then festival organiser, 1993. (Jan McMillan)

On the Saturday night the Mushy Pea Theatre Company, a group of Oxford teenagers directed by Humphrey Carpenter, performed a tribute to the young Judy Garland. Humphrey had first come to the festival in 1986 to talk about his book on American writers in Paris. At that time he was already established as the biographer of Auden, Tolkien and Pound, but his passion was for his new jazz band, Vile Bodies. He rang Alan Hancox to ask if he could bring them to the festival, and was delighted by his immediate and

Humphrey Carpenter (in striped shirt) leads 'The Festival Allstars' into the next number, 1994. (Jan McMillan)

positive response. It was Alan's openness to ideas, his allowing people to be creative in their own way, that Humphrey had in the back of his mind when he accepted the festival's invitation to direct 1994.

Richard Cohen's big box office successes had made him a hard act to follow. Humphrey, performer as well as writer, decided he would put his energies into making it as uniquely alive as he could. His first step was to invite Ralph Steadman to be artist-in-residence. Humphrey wanted an 'explosive and stimulating' festival? For the front of the brochure Ralph drew a multi-coloured explosion of firework-like creativity rearing over the Pittville Pump Room. He set the Youth Drama Festival on to his book *I Leonardo*, which resulted in an extraordinary collaboration between the National Star Centre, the nearby college for disabled students, and the Cheltenham and Gloucestershire College of Higher Education. During the festival itself – when not on stage, which he frequently was – Ralph would be making 'Paranoids', manipulating polaroids into fantastical psycho-portraits of the speakers. He wrote to Humphrey afterwards (the pot to the kettle) 'What a festival! – and fuelled by your manic energy (which) drove us all onwards at an alarming rate. I just wanted to thank you for including me in your madness. It was a great privilege to meet all those creative souls and have them at my mercy for five minutes.'

One of those souls was Alan Bennett, who submitted to the shenanigans of photos and fans with amiable patience. After a sell-out reading of his *Diaries*, he signed books literally for hours, drawing a little picture of himself for each recipient.

One of the themes was 'science writing', a day devoted to the new wave of popular

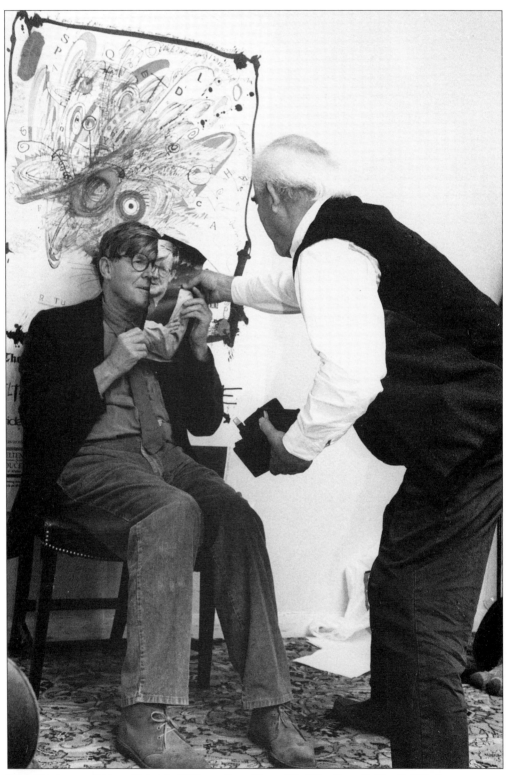

Ralph Steadman, artist-in-residence for 1994, creating a 'Paranoid' of Alan Bennett. (Jan McMillan)

science books. The co-discoverer of DNA, James D. Watson, came over from the States to discuss the ethics of genetic engineering with British neuroscientist Steven Rose. Douglas Adams and Richard Dawkins talking about Darwin, is there a God?, and other mysteries of the universe were so fascinating that they ran over by an hour or more. It was a day that achieved that magic fusion of participants eager to hear and meet each other and an audience excited to witness the results.

One of the revivals was the Festival Club, presided over by Marcus Moore, who emerged from his existing role as co-ordinator of the Youth Drama Festival to reveal himself a performance poet and inimitable master of ceremonies for late-night music and word sessions in the Pillar Room bar. Humphrey's contacts on BBC radio brought *Book at Bedtime* to the Festival Club, from where it was broadcast live for two years. He remembers Edwina Currie mustering a rather small audience at the front and telling them they must clap fast to make themselves sound larger.

One of the innovations was the '1894 Booker Prize', an idea repeated annually ever since under the chairmanship of the publisher Ion Trewin. That year it took place in a marquee at the back of the Town Hall, adopted for a couple of years – after the style of Hay and Edinburgh – to cope with large numbers. After the panel – Melvyn Bragg, Victoria Glendinning, Books Page editor of the *Daily Telegraph* John Coldstream, Cambridge academic Gillian Beer and Booker Prize organiser Martyn Goff – had discussed their six novels with flair and erudition, they retired while Humphrey turned to the audience for their opinions and vote. Egged on by his urging, excitement mounted. I rushed to and fro bearing news from either front, and finally audience and panel each elected a winner.

Humphrey's articulate enthusiasm, his skill on stage – as interviewer, chairman, introducer or plain animateur – made him instantly popular with the Cheltenham audiences. He was completely delighted by the experience: 'It's like ones wedding day, but it goes on and on.' A motion was moved in the House of Commons by the local MP and recorded in Hansard: 'That this House applauds the success of the 1994 Cheltenham Festival of Literature under the inspired direction of Mr Humphrey Carpenter.'

He was keen to go on for another two years, despite the enormous amount of work that the festival always entails. For 1995 he commissioned Posy Simmonds as festival artist. For the first time a primary school participated in the Youth Drama Festival: Horsley Primary School performed a musical version of her story *Fred*, pop idol and cat, featuring a giant catflap and a massive all-singing, all-dancing under-eleven cast. Posy's drawings wittily took up the major theme of the festival, 'In Search of an Enemy', which brought nineteen authors from Central and Eastern Europe to talk about what it was like to be a writer in a post-ideological society.

Agony to have to leave out so much, so many excellent readings and talks, performances and discussions; not to acknowledge the names and achievements of

Dave Hedley-Wood and Simon Arinze, two of the many Town Hall staff who help to make the festival happen, 1993.
(Jan McMillan)

writers who may not be known to the reader; not to go into the panoply of activities organised by the Festivals' Education Officer – a post inaugurated in 1993 with the support of Martin Davis and the Summerfield Trust, and South West Arts – for schools and groups all over the county; or to describe the camaraderie that develops over the ten days of the festival between the regulars in the audience and the organisers.

But I cannot leave out the first United Kingdom Allcomers' Poetry Slam, started by Marcus Moore after he had taken part in one at Glastonbury Festival the year before. 'Every poet in the realm, from slam champion to brave beginner, is invited to stand and deliver' reads the invitation in the brochure. And they did, not just London clubbers with face furniture, but retired postmen with anarchic souls. Heat after heat, judged by audience and panel and compèred by slam veteran Thom the World Poet, were whistled and clapped until we got the winner of the night.

The audience for the Slam streamed through the crowds waiting to get their books signed by Seamus Heaney, another immortal moment in the history of the festival. He had just been awarded the Nobel Prize. Cheltenham, his old stamping ground, was his first public appearance. There was a press conference. The mayor presented him with a china goblet that he forgot to take home. When he entered the Main Hall, the crowd rose as one to give him a standing ovation. Heaney had a sore arm that meant he feared he could sign books afterwards for only a limited time, but in the end he insisted on going on to the end, a couple of hours at least.

And Humphrey, among others, insists that I must not leave out the behind-the-scenes staff: the box office staff on duty from morning to night and more, the attendants who move chairs and staging in and out of rooms at breakneck speed, then change their clothes and demeanour to show people to their seats, the annual influx of festival helpers, usually between school and university, called on for anything and everything. And at last the sound in the main hall is as good as it ever can be – thanks to the expertise of the current sound engineers, the installation of thick curtaining (first recommended in 1950), and tickets not sold for bad spots.

Many of the behind-the-scenes areas had been my responsibility, but in 1995 I was given the chance of directing the following year's festival with Humphrey Carpenter, supported by my successor Sarah Smyth, whose immaculate efficiency I was particularly well-placed to appreciate. I made my speciality 'women and writing' which allowed me to invite some of my favourite

Marcus Moore. (Christopher Cornwell)

speakers back – Hermione Lee, Michèle Roberts, Jean Binta Breeze, Beryl Bainbridge, Susan Hill, U.A. Fanthorpe, Jenny Joseph, Ursula Owen, Lisa Jardine, Shirley Hughes, Hilary Spurling – as well as authors less familiar to Cheltenham, Mavis Gallant, Nell Dunn and Grace Paley among them.

That year Humphrey, always visible in the media, was hot news. His biography of Robert Runcie with its controversial revelations about the Wales marriage had just come out and was making the front pages. He had created another hard act to follow.

Annette Kobak, writer and reviewer, then resident in Cheltenham and chairman of the Management Committee, was the one who thought to ask John Walsh, whose charismatic eloquence she had seen displayed at Hay when he was literary editor of the *Sunday Times*. John had moved to the *Independent*, where he is assistant editor. He remembers setting out his ideas before the Committee: a celebration of Irish writing, a commemoration of Indian Independence and – here his words slowed beneath a weight of images – the Age of Decadence . . . white lilies, the fume of incense, doomed suicidal poets, absinthe sullen on café tables, Baudelaire and Verlaine . . . 'Mr Walsh', he was interrupted, 'Mr Walsh, have you any idea of the price of lilies?'

The *Independent* together with Ireland's *Sunday Independent*, decided to come in as the festival's main sponsor, and together they put the full force of their editorial coverage behind the 1997 festival. John was determined, as he put it, 'to go for broke', and create a programme that embraced the whole culture of the printed word, containing every kind of book and beyond, 'as in a good eclectic literary page'.

Unlike Humphrey, who was keen to keep the focus of the festival inside the Town Hall, John wanted to spread it through the streets of Cheltenham. Street theatre on the

Some of the festival directors involved in the 1999 Anniversary Festival. Front row, left to right: Sarah Smyth, Elizabeth Ja Howard, Nicola Bennett, Shelagh Hancox. Middle row: Ion Trewin (chair of the Festival Committee), Humphrey Carpen Ronald Harwood, A.C.H. Smith, Ian Hamilton. Back row: Melvyn Bragg (for Alan Hancox), John Walsh, Richard Cohen a Lawrence Sail. (Susan Greenhill)

Promenade, a giant book in Imperial Gardens, talks in the Library and Art Gallery, poetry in the upper room of Peppers Bar, free music in O'Hagans, story-telling in the Playhouse theatre. The idea, as the indefatigable Marcus Moore who organises it tells me, is to fit performer to venue: like Adrian Henri who loves to perform in a small relaxed clubby space, but rarely get the chance to see anything but a large hall.

O'Hagans was the place the weekend the Irish were in town. Lunchtime fiddle music helped to pack it on Saturday and then the momentum was all its own. Edna O'Brien, Clare Boylan, Colm Tóibín, Paul Durcan, John Banville and many more. Talk and more talk, John Walsh – charming and loquacious, dressed in a series of lollipop-coloured jackets – miraculously omnipresent, Joyce and Yeats the presiding spirits, another of those times when the magic rolls.

Among discussions of the fading Raj, contemporary Indian writers introduced themselves to Cheltenham audiences in a series of events through the week, although Arundhati Roy needed no introduction on the eve of her Booker success, and Salman Rushdie could not afford to be introduced, but slipped in to join them all for a final summarising.

The festival had yet again moved into a higher gear. Box office soared. And 1998 was the same story. Rock 'n' Roll Day brought the highest audiences ever, not necessarily for rock events (Terry Pratchett, Helen Fielding on 'Bridget Jones', Raymond Blanc), but Ian Dury talking to John Walsh about his lyrics – not poetry, he insisted, songs – and life was generally agreed to be the big moment of the day.

'The audience *loved* it. They lapped it up.' In his second year, this is what Walsh came to understand and enjoy most about the festival: the sense that he could pick up what the audience was feeling and steer the event accordingly, and give it outline. Like all the directors, he has a great deal of respect for the 'Cheltenham audience'. He cites David Lodge, Beryl Bainbridge, Richard Holmes and Orlando Figes as among the writers who have commented to him personally on the level of readership and the perspicacity of questioners.

For 1999 twelve former directors have assembled under the guiding hand of Sarah Smyth, responsible for organising not only them but the entire proceedings, to create a festival they hope will be worthy of the 50th birthday.

After that, who knows? . . .

Our world in 1999 is very different from that of 1949. Spoken word events are so popular that bookshops are being opened with custom-made auditoria inside. Publishers build author tours into the launch of a book. All the razzmatazz and money would astonish John Moore if he came back today. But he would recognise that curious interaction between speaker and audience. He would know that moment when the prosaic becomes poetic, when one wants to be nowhere else because it is happening now, here – as alive and unique as a football match, or a concert, or a stage performance. He would be pleased, or perhaps amused, that so many of the features and ideas that he and Robert Henriques espoused have resurfaced down the years, sometimes forgotten and reinvented, sometimes the basis of a constant tradition. And he would know that in the beginning and the end, the whole edifice rests on the writers who give up their time and solitude to appear in public, some eagerly, some nervously, but usually with a sense of pleasure that there are people out there who like their books and want to hear them.

ACKNOWLEDGEMENTS

My first thanks go to the directors of past festivals and their representatives: Lucile Bell (John Moore), Humphrey Carpenter, his wife Mari and daughter Clare, Richard Cohen, Nest Cleverdon (Douglas Cleverdon), Veronica Gosling (Robert Henriques), Ian Hamilton, Shelagh Hancox (Alan Hancox), Ronald Harwood, Elizabeth Jane Howard, Paul Humphreys and his wife Eileen, P.J. Kavanagh and his wife Kate, Gordon Parsons and his wife Ann, Lawrence Sail, A.C.H. Smith and John Walsh. Generous with their time and memories, they made my task as interviewer a pleasure.

My next are for the following individuals for their festival recollections: Jill Balcon, Melvyn Bragg, Elizabeth Browning, Alan Brownjohn, John Coldstream, Joy Coombes, Charles Fisher, Barbara Hooper, Jenery Howard, Richard Last, Heather Newman, Sonia Rolt, Alan Tucker, Marilyn Warnick, Don and Maisie Weekes, Tudor Williams, Joan Wilder and Brian Wynn.

Research has taken me to several organisations whose staff have been most helpful in fulfilling my requests. I am grateful to: Steven Blake of Cheltenham Art Gallery and Museum; Annette White of Cheltenham Borough Council; Anthony Lyons and Tim Pearse of Cheltenham College; Roger Beacham and staff at Cheltenham Library; Aylwin Sampson of Cheltenham Local History Society; Rachel Stafford at the Everyman Theatre; Andrew Holiday at Gloucester Local Studies Library; Anita Syvret and Sue Robins at the *Gloucestershire Echo*; Vicky Thorpe at Gloucestershire Record Office; Gayle M. Barkley of Huntington Library, California; John Shakles of the John Moore Society; Michael Bott of University of Reading Library (Robert Henriques archive) and Tia O'Rourke at the Savile Club.

I am indebted to Cheltenham Arts Festivals for allowing me to dig through the records of the Literature Festival, and to those who have worked for the festival in a professional capacity and shared their experiences with me, namely: Ann Marie Dabrowska, Michael Darling, John Haynes, Victoria Millar, Marcus Moore, Michael Rayward and Jeremy Tyndall. Special thanks go to those in the Literature Festival office, particularly Sarah Smyth, whose sustained support has been invaluable, and Kate Murray-Smith for her research assistance.

For permission to quote from letters and unpublished writings my thanks go to Jill Balcon (C. Day Lewis), Lucile Bell (John Moore), Richard Boston, Veronica Gosling (Robert Henriques), Shelagh Hancox (Alan Hancox), Elizabeth Jane Howard, P.J. Kavanagh, Cathy Lee (Laurie Lee), the Trustees of the Estate of Philip Larkin, and Ralph Steadman. Letters to Elizabeth Jane Howard from Henry Green (EJH 759), Laurie Lee (EJH 1180) and Eric Linklater (EJH 1215) are published by permission of the Huntington Library, San Marino, California. My thanks and apologies also extend to any copyright holders whom I have been unable to trace in the time available.

I have received much valued editorial advice from Ion Trewin and Richard Cohen, not to mention Anne Bennett and Jaqueline Mitchell of Sutton Publishing.

And my last thanks are saved for my husband Will and son Joe who cheerfully put up with a six-month invasion by paper.